Building a Noble World

Shiv R. Jhawar

Building a Noble World

FIRST EDITION: October 2004

Website: www.nobleworld.org
Email: order@nobleworld.org

ISBN 0-9749197-0-5

Published by:
SRJ Consulting
Post Box 2998, Chicago, IL 60690-2998 USA

Credits for permission to reproduce copyright photographs:

Photograph of Swami Muktananda is Copyright © 2004 SYDA Foundation®

Photograph of Paramahansa Yogananda, 1924, is courtesy of Self-Realization Fellowship.

Photograph of Swami Sivananda is courtesy of Divine Life Society.

Photograph of Shiv R. Jhawar with Swami Muktananda is Copyright © 2004 Noble World Foundation.

All pictorial illustrations are Copyright © 2004 Noble World Foundation.

PRINTED AND BOUND IN THE UNITED STATES OF AMERICA.

Disclaimer: Unless otherwise noted, the views, opinions, and conclusions expressed in this book are solely those of the author and are not necessarily those of the spiritual masters quoted in this book.

Table of Contents

The author bowing before Baba Muktananda in 1974

Dedication

With my heart full of gratitude, I dedicate this book to the sacred memory of Baba Muktananda, the *Parama Siddha* (supremely powerful spiritual master), who gave the world the following message:

> Understand your Self.
> See your Self.
> Seek your Self, and find your Self.
> Hari, Shiva, Shakti, Allah, Jesus, Buddha — all dwell within you.
> Kneel to your own Self.
> Honor and worship your own Self.
> Meditate on your own Self.
> God dwells within you as You.

Swami Muktananda (1908–1982)

In Memory of
Swami Muktananda

Swami Muktananda (1908–1982), known worldwide as Baba Muktananda, was the foremost disciple and successor of Bhagwan Nityananda (1896–1961) of Ganeshpuri, India. Bhagwan Nityananda was a supreme *avadhuta* (extraordinary being) who was always in bliss.

Both the East and the West regarded Baba Muktananda as the Guru's Guru (*param siddha*) because he was highly revered by many yoga masters. In his spiritual autobiography, *Play of Consciousness*, Baba disclosed his own mysterious spiritual experiences. During a conversation with Dr. William Tiller, professor of Physics at Stanford University, Baba commented: "I am speaking from my direct observation, and I have described these things systematically and at length in my book, *Play of Consciousness*. Most saints keep all these details very secret, but I have been compelled to disclose them to the whole world."[a]

Revealing Baba Muktananda's marvelous power to transmit a spiritual experience at will, Swami Chidvilasananda, the current head of the Siddha Yoga lineage, wrote: "At one point during the *pattabhisheka*, the ceremony during which Baba Muktananda passed on to me the power of his lineage, he whispered *soham* and *aham Brahmasmi* in my ear. I experienced the mantra as an immensely powerful force which rocketed at lightning speed throughout my bloodstream and created an upheaval in my entire system. I instantly transcended body-consciousness and became aware that all distinctions such as inner and outer were false and artificial. Everything was the same; what was within me was also without. My mind became completely blank. There was only the pulsating awareness 'I am That,' accompanied by great bliss and light. When my mind again began to function, all I could think was, 'What is Baba? Who is this being who looks so ordinary, yet has the

---

[a] *In the Company of a Siddha; Interviews and Conversations with Swami Muktananda*, a talk with Dr. William Tiller, professor of Physics at Stanford University, (Oakland, California, SYDA Foundation, 1978), p. 129.

capacity to transmit such an experience at will?'"[b]

Who is Baba Muktanada? In his own words: "I am what you see. If you see me as an individual, I am an individual. If you see me as a human being, I am a human being. If you see me as a fool, I am a fool. If you see me as a yogi, I am a yogi, and if you see me as a realized being, I am a realized being. It all depends upon you. I look at myself being aware that I am—I am. Yes, I am That. That 'I' has a great meaning, that 'I' is Consciousness."[c]

In *Secret of the Siddhas*, Baba traced his lineage to Lord Shiva, the original Guru: "From Shiva came Vasugupta, Somananda, Utpalacharya, Lakshmanagupta, Ramakantha, Abhinavagupta, Kshemaraja, Yogaraja, Kallata, Pradyumna Bhatta, Prajnarjuna, Mahadev Bhatta, Srikantha Bhatta, Bhaskara, and other Siddhas." Baba continued: "Ishwara Iyer was a great yogi who had practiced austerities. He was an enlightened Siddha Guru....The one who loved him above all was Nityananda." Thus, other Siddha Gurus include recent perfect masters such as Ishwara Iyer and his disciple, Nityananda of Ganeshpuri.

The true Guru (called Sadguru) is the Power that never dies. *Shiva Sutra Vimarshini*, an authoritative scripture of Kashmir Shaivism, states: "Guru paramesvari anugrahika shakti," which defines a true Guru as "the grace-bestowing power (*shakti*) of God." Just as milk can be transferred from one vessel to another, so also the grace-bestowing power is transferred in a Guru-disciple succession. The ancient lineage continues to this day through Swami Chidvilasananda (better known as Gurumayi) who embodies this Power of Guruhood.

[b]Swami Muktananda, *I am That*, Preface by Swami Chidvilasananda (South Fallsburg, New York: SYDA Foundation, 1992), p. xxiii.
[c]Swami Muktananda, *From the Finite to the Infinite Volume II*, Chapter "Death of the Ego" (South Fallsburg, New York: SYDA Foundation, 1989), p. 332.

Author's Acknowledgements

There are many dear and near ones who have helped me with their timely suggestions and encouragement. Let me thank all of you with these words: "O divine Consciousness in you! I bow again and again to Thee as my heart wells up in love for Thee."

In order to facilitate reading of this book, I have quoted the works of many great beings including Patanjali, Swami Muktananda, Swami Chidvilasananda, Swami Rama Tirtha, Ramakrishna Paramahansa, Swami Vivekananda, Yogananda Paramahansa, Swami Sivananda of Rishikesh, Swami Satyananda, Swami Vishnu Tirtha, Kabir, Anandmayi, Aurobindo of Pondicherry, Sri Chinmoy, Nisargadatta Maharaj, Narayan Swami of Muzzafarnagar, Swami Lakshman Joo, Swami Prabhupada, Mahatma Gandhi, Jawaharlal Nehru, Abraham Lincoln, John Woodroffe, Albert Einstein, Carl Jung, Dalai Lama, Jimmy Carter, Kofi Annan, Martin Luther King, Jr., Herman Hesse, and others. I offer my gratitude to all great beings whose blessings are ever lasting.

In the course of writing this book — while meditating one day — I saw myself standing before Gurumayi Chidvilasananda while her right hand extended to rest on my heart. Instantly, my eyes closed and blissful tears trickled down, offering my reverence for her blessing.

I hope you enjoy reading this book as much as I have enjoyed writing it. If this book proves instrumental in changing your outlook on life, thank all-pervading Consciousness whom I call Baba Muktananda. As stated in this book, on Monday, September 16, 1974, I received *something* from Baba — something so precious that all the honor and remembrance I can give him is not enough.

—**Shiv R. Jhawar**
October 28, 2004

Shiv R. Jhawar

About the Author

Raised in India, Shiv R. Jhawar came to the United States in 1973 to pursue higher studies in Accounting. While living in Chicago, he met Swami Muktananda, an eminent yogi and celebrated author of *Play of Consciousness*. Recalling the divine experience of *shaktipat* initiation from Swami Muktananda on September 16, 1974, he remarked, "Once you have an experience of transcendental reality, you are changed forever." Humility is the highest watermark in spirituality. He lives a simple life dedicated to Swami Muktananda's teaching: "To honor the inner Self is to serve me."

The author is a Chartered Accountant by profession. He holds a Master's degree in Accounting from the University of Illinois at Urbana-Champaign. After qualifying as an Enrolled Agent to practice before the Internal Revenue Service in 1978, he has been practicing tax accounting in Chicago. His article "International Dimensions of Auditing" was published in the *Chartered Accountant* (September 1973) and the *International Accountant* (December 1973). He also served as a lecturer at colleges in both India and the U.S.A.

Gifted with the ability to communicate deep spiritual concepts clearly, the author delivers lectures in the U.S.A. and abroad. The ideas presented in *Building a Noble World* not only inspire people to intensify their spiritual growth, but also promote peace, harmony, and well-being in the world.

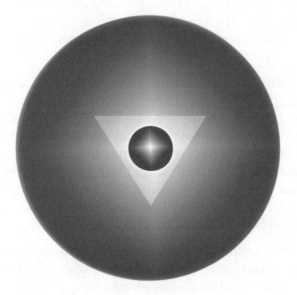

Blue light

Invocation

As I begin this work, I prostrate first to the true Guru and recite the following verse:

अकथादि त्रिरेखाब्जे सहस्रदलमण्डले ।

हंसपार्श्वत्रिकोणे च स्मरेत्तन्मघ्यगं गुरुम ॥ ५८ ॥

akathadi trirekhabje, sahsradala mandale /
hansa parshva trikone cha, smaret tanmadhyagam gurum // 58 //

"In the *sahasrara* (the luminous center in the brain), there exists a triangle. The true Guru (also called *Sadguru* or *Satguru*) lives in the middle of this triangle in the form of a blue light. Remember this inner Guru."

— *Sri Guru Gita*, a sacred hymn in the *Skanda Purana*

Sadgurunath Maharaj ki Jay!

(Hail to the true Guru!)

Introduction

By J. V. Lakshmana Rao
Managing Editor, *India Tribune,* Chicago

The world has been passing through very difficult times. Political and religious conflicts between countries and people are seen everywhere. However, the fight against terrorism has brought most nations together. There is unanimity among many major right thinking countries to fight against the evil forces of terrorism.

India was perhaps the first country to suffer the onslaught of terrorism. But the real unified fight against terrorism has been launched only after the September 11, 2001, incidents in the United States. It was India that had first voluntarily offered its help and cooperation to the United States when the superpower announced that it would fight the menace. India knows about the intensity of the problem because its people have been suffering from cross-border terrorism.

India has been a spiritual light of the world for centuries. It is one of the world's oldest surviving civilizations, despite the fact that it has suffered the onslaughts of several foreign invasions. There is historic evidence to show that the Indian subcontinent existed as a unified country of several princely states centuries ago. However, invasions had disintegrated the subcontinent into several small countries. Spiritually, these smaller countries still share the same ethos.

The idea mooted by the author in the unification of these smaller neighboring countries with India, and calling it the "Indus Union," is definitely a solution for the peaceful coexistence of people. The prosperity of the United States of America is a practical example for such a unified country. Smaller countries are economically weak, and politically unstable. Ethnic conflicts are ruining their economy. Their resources are not comprehensive enough for the sustenance of their people. But as a unified political and economic unit, these countries can share their resources. It is not necessary that each country should give up its individuality, identity, or sovereignty. The European Union is a good example of how this can work.

Unification is possible if human beings shed their hatred for each other. Fruits of universal love can be shared only when people become spiritually conscious. This, however, does not mean that they give up their respective religions. They can become spiritually stronger by retaining their religious identities and by sharing their love for their peaceful coexistence. India has always believed in such philosophy and propagated such thought. Indian philosophy is ancient; it has survived several ages because of its clarity and universality. There is no history to suggest that India had ever invaded another country or tried to expand its territory, nor did it make efforts to spread its religious faith.

The book, *Building a Noble World,* is not just about religion and spirituality. It is about practical life and unification of humanity that leads to world peace. It dwells on varied subjects such as religion, spirituality, unification of the Indian subcontinent as a harbinger of world unification, the author's own experience of *shaktipat,* and the understanding of yoga.

Today, the world has recognized the importance of the Vedas, their underlying philosophy, yoga, and the technique of meditation. More and more people are practicing yoga for its uniqueness, efficacy, and simplicity. The West is looking toward the Vedic and yogic philosophy of India for peace, prosperity, and universal brotherhood. It is in the effort of spreading spirituality and sharing universal brotherhood that this book is relevant. The author is a spiritual person of exemplary simplicity. He lives a simple, ordinary life, practicing the high ideals of spirituality and yoga. Indeed, he is a blessed human being and a practical philosopher. Though the author makes his living as a chartered accountant, he sets a remarkable example of how spirituality can be practiced.

This thought-provoking book, interspersed with highly

knowledgeable quotes from the writings of distinguished spiritual masters, will stimulate the intellect of those who read it. I am confident all will benefit from it. It is hoped that it will help promote peace and brotherhood among all human beings.

It is my conviction that this book releases tremendous force that may ultimately help build a nobler world.

—J. V. Lakshmana Rao, Managing Editor,
India Tribune, Chicago

J. V. Lakshmana Rao is currently serving as the managing editor of the *India Tribune*, published from Chicago, New York, and Atlanta. He also holds a part-time teaching position in the Medill School of Journalism, Northwestern University, Evanston, Illinois. As a veteran journalist, Lakshmana Rao has worked for several leading English daily newspapers in India, and published thousands of articles concerning politics, spirituality, religion, culture, and art. During his 35-year-long journalistic career, he has interviewed a number of noted world figures. He has received several prestigious awards, and he has been honored by several social and cultural organizations. He strongly believes that world peace and harmony can be achieved by working toward unification through political, spiritual, and cultural processes. He has been acclaimed as a prolific writer and respected columnist.

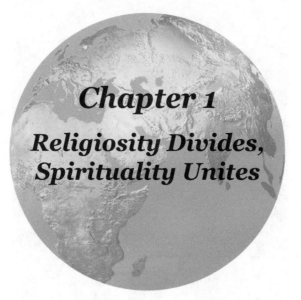

Chapter 1

Religiosity Divides, Spirituality Unites

Albert Einstein (1879–1955)

CHAPTER 1
Religiosity Divides, Spirituality Unites

Never before has there been a greater need for global harmony among people and nations than now. Modern nuclear weapons are many times more dangerous than the atomic bombs of the Second World War. Nuclear weapons have the potential of destroying most life on Earth. What could be a greater nightmare than having nuclear weapons in the hands of terrorists? Who could have imagined the complete destruction of the twin towers of the World Trade Center — the icon of foreign trade — until the deadly attacks of September 11, 2001? The risks of terrorism cannot be ignored.

Albert Einstein (1879–1955), a German-born American physicist who discovered the theory of atomic energy, signed the famous "**Russell-Einstein Manifesto**" before he died on April 18, 1955. The Russell-Einstein Manifesto was issued on July 9, 1955 in London. The Manifesto called upon scientists to engage in the public debate on the horrors facing humanity as a result of scientific and technological developments. The manifesto concluded: "There lies before us, if we choose, continued progress in happiness, knowledge, and wisdom. Shall we instead choose death, because we cannot forget our quarrels? We appeal, as human beings, to human beings: remember your humanity and forget the rest. If you can do so, the way lies open to a new Paradise; if you cannot, there lies before you the risk of universal death."

In this nuclear age, wars, violence, prejudices, hatred, suffering, death, and destruction are bound to continue until humanity dispels the illusion of separation.

1. The Absolute Can Only Be One

The most serious rifts in the world tend to be religious.

The world's top nine religions are Christianity (33%), Islam (20%), Hinduism (13%), Buddhism (6%), Sikhism (0.4%), Judaism (0.2%), Baha'ism (0.1%), Confucianism (0.1%), and Jainism (0.1%).

Throughout history, many religions have caused separation among people and nations by differentiating between "our God" and "their God." God is conceived of as an omniscient, omnipotent, and omnipresent super conscious Spirit of the universe. Therefore, God is Absolute Reality and the absolute can only be one. From the point of view of the Absolute Reality, individuals are not separate from one another. Just as the ocean underlies all its different waves, so also the same Absolute Reality underlies all its religions. Muslims call the Absolute, Allah; Hindus call the Absolute, *Ishwara*[d]; and Christians call the Absolute, God—all these names point to the same Absolute Reality, which is the nameless experience. In fact, the Absolute Reality is the total cosmic consciousness. Allah is that supreme Consciousness which is omnipresent, omnipotent, and omniscient as is the Tao of Lao-tse, the Nirvana of Buddha, the Jehovah of Moses, the Father of Jesus, or the primordial sound Om of the Vedas. When it is fully understood that the Absolute can only be one, a person may follow one religion but will have respect for all other religions.

To disrespect other religions is to disrespect one's own God because it is the same God that is worshipped in all religions. Any place of worship, regardless of its religious label, must invoke a spirit of humanism. Therefore, anyone, regardless of caste, class, age, sex, or nationality, should be able to visit such a place. A religion becomes humanitarian when it welcomes everyone to its place of worship.

Science may not include the concept of God, but it cannot deny the existence of energy. *Webster's Concise Dictionary*

---

[d] The three major gods called *Brahma* (creation), *Vishnu* (preservation), and *Shiva* (destruction) are, in fact, different functions of the same God, and are named accordingly. God the Father is equivalent to *Ishwara*, God the Son to the Guru, and God the Holy Ghost to the *Atman* (inner Self).

defines God as, "The Supreme Being, creator and ruler of the universe, conceived of as eternal, omniscient, good, and almighty." Thus, God is eternal and, therefore, indestructible. According to modern science, energy is indestructible. The Law of Conservation of Energy specifically states that energy cannot be created or destroyed, but it can only be changed from one form to another. There is no destruction, only transformation. Matter and energy appear to be two, but they are convertible into each other. Albert Einstein's famous equation[e] $E=Mc^2$ proves that matter can be reconverted into energy. Matter is another form of energy just as ice is another form of water.

The Law of Conservation of Energy is the very basis of modern theories such as Albert Einstein's Theory of Relativity and Max Planck's Quantum Theory. In fact, this energy is the root cause of every action in this universe. According to modern science, the same energy manifests as light, heat, electricity, magnetism, and sound, and they are inter-convertible. Indeed, this energy is all pervading in different forms and names.

2. Religiosity Is Not Spirituality

The indestructible essence of this energy is called Spirit. One who realizes or identifies oneself as Spirit is spiritual. Just as gold is not affected by the different forms it is shaped into, so also the inner Spirit remains unaffected by its outer names and forms. It is this common inner Spirit that unites us all in spite of our outer differences. Spirit is universal. Truly, there is one Spirit hidden in all beings. Turning within to become aware of the indwelling Spirit is spirituality. In so practicing spirituality, there is no distinction of caste or creed, sect or religion, age or sex.

---

[e] According to Albert Einstein's Special Theory of Relativity, matter is a form of energy that can be reconverted into energy. In $E=Mc^2$, the "c" stands for the velocity of light—186,300 miles a second. Multiply c^2 by the amount of matter "M" to get the amount of energy "E."

Religiosity refers to different dogmas, rituals, and customs in which a particular religion is presented. Spirituality, being a universal principle, addresses the intrinsic nature of the individual, whereas religiosity addresses external behavior. A person may be formally religious, yet may or may not practice spirituality. Thus, being religious is not necessarily the same as being spiritual.

If spirituality were practiced sincerely, one would rise above all religious barriers, expanding the Self to embrace all humanity, even all creation. Religiosity divides, spirituality unites. Speaking of superficial differences among religious followers, **Yogananda** (1893–1952), the prominent Indian spiritual master who took up permanent residence in the United States, rightly remarked: "These differences in perception are the cause of arguments and controversies, each seeing only a part of the whole truth. An exchange of differing views is constructive if done with openness and respect; but destructive, ending in quarrels, if there is bigotry and fanaticism."[1]

The same Spirit is at the core of every human being. The ultimate aim of all human beings is the same: to avoid pain and acquire happiness. We all have the same digestive, respiratory, and blood circulatory systems. The color of our blood is the same. We all eat, drink, endure pain, enjoy pleasure, and eventually die. The feeling of love or anger is the same in all of us. The relationship that one individual has with another is through the same universal energy. "Like attracts like" is the Law of Affinity. Accordingly, we ought to live in harmony with one another.

Only when we realize spirituality, can we live peacefully with people of other religions. No one is born into this world with a religion engraved on his or her skin, nor can people take their religion with them when they die. Everyone is a human being first. Religion is thrust on a person in between birth and death. In fact, the names of various religions are like badges that students wear to indicate the various educational institutions to which they belong. It is sheer identification with a particular religious label that has been responsible for conflicts among various religious groups.

Since all prophets were the messengers of but one God, they preached love for the one and same God. **The feeling of oneness is defined as love.** We love our family members because we feel a sense of oneness with them. Similarly, to fully love the all-pervading God, one must feel the sense of oneness with all. Without this feeling of oneness with all, can God be said to have been truly loved?

Love expresses a human being's inner purity — often through tearful emotions. **Anandamayi** (1896–1981), one of the prominent saints of India, was once asked:

"What is the easiest way to God?"

"Profuse tears," she replied.

"And if tears do not come?"

"Then you should seek the company of those who shed tears, namely in *satsang* [company of holy beings]. This is the easiest way to God, through love and devotion."[2]

The essence of every religion is love. If a religion teaches hatred for other religions, it is not a religion; it is anti-religion. In the words of **Rama Tirtha** (1873–1906), one of the greatest spiritual masters of India: "The religion, which is not tolerant or liberal enough to preach love, and live in peace with others, is no religion. It is simple immorality, narrow-mindedness, orthodoxy, and bigotry."[3]

3. The True Meaning of "I Am the Only God"

Religion itself is not God; it is only a path that leads to God. Different prophets have laid down different paths to reach the same God who is eternal, immortal, indivisible, and limitless. Every prophet preaches according to the time, place, and prevailing conditions. A comparative study of the scriptures of different religions would reveal that, despite widespread differences among their doctrines, mythology, forms, rituals, and ceremonies, all religions are one in Spirit. In reality, these religions complement, rather than contradict one another. For example, photographs of the sun taken from various locations or at different times of day look different, yet it is the same sun in all the photographs. The sooner religious people look upon all religions as equal and thus put aside their superficial differences, the more this world will benefit.

Those who claim that following their religion or its founder is the only path to know God might reflect on this: Who was God before the birth of the founder of their religion? Few people realize that the teachings of a particular prophet did not become a religion until after his death. For instance, **Jesus Christ** (4 BC–A.D. 30) was not a "Christian" by birth; he was a Jew born in present day Israel. Jesus Christ did not create the Christian religion. Long after Jesus was crucified, his followers created the Christian religion by proclaiming Jesus as its founder. Similarly, Siddharta Gautama, known as **Gautama Buddha** (560 BC–480 BC), was not a "Buddhist" by birth; he was a Hindu born in India. Buddha did not create the Buddhist religion. Hundreds of years after Buddha died, his followers created the Buddhist religion by proclaiming Buddha as its founder.

A particular follower of a religion may believe that his path is the only valid path to God, but to God, all paths are valid. For example, a tenant in a large apartment building may consider the apartment he lives in as his own, while remaining unconcerned with the other apartments in the building. However, the owner of the building regards all apartments in the building as his own. Similarly, God regards all religions as His own. Jesus, Muhammad, Rama, Krishna, Buddha, Mahavira, Zoroaster, and Guru Nanak, to name a few, are worthy of our reverence because all of them had direct experience of the ever-blissful state of the same Universal Spirit.

The ultimate statement "I am the only way" or "I am the only God" causes confusion to many. The question arises, for example, if Jesus is considered the only God then how can Buddha also be considered the only God? The answer lies in this analogy: When a river merges into the vast ocean, it loses its identification as a river. Then, the river's declaration "I am the ocean" becomes true. Similarly, when a prophet merges his sense of individuality with the all-pervasive Consciousness, his declaration "I am the only God" is entirely true. As far as the ultimate realization of every founder of a religion is concerned, it is the attainment of the same Absolute Reality. It is for this reason that the title Christ conveys exactly the same universal consciousness as does the title Buddha.

Every great being established in the Universal Consciousness of "I am God" can be proclaimed as the Son of God, in the sense that the grace bestowing power of God freely and fully works through that great being. If an ordinary human being can have many children, why cannot God have many children? **Muktananda** (1908–1982), one of the greatest spiritual masters of India, wrote: "Many religious groups claim that theirs is the only path to the Truth. The Hare Krishna people claim that one cannot be redeemed unless one believes in Krishna. Muslims claim that one cannot be redeemed unless one has faith in the Koran. Christians claim that one cannot be redeemed unless one follows Christ. The followers of other religions make similar statements. But God never made an agreement with any of these religions. All religions are of fairly recent origin, but God existed since the beginning of time. He would not have signed a contract with any religious founder saying, 'You are my exclusive salesman.' The significance of a religion is its emphasis on turning within, not the belief of some of its members that it is better than other religions."[4]

Each religion arose according to its own time and culture, and each one represents a great truth. Humanity will be greatly benefited if religions focus on creating more saintly people rather than creating more temples, mosques, monasteries, synagogues, or churches.

4. As You Sow, So Shall You Reap

The fundamental teaching of all religions is to do good to others. People sow their deeds and reap their fruits. Anyone who does harm is repaid in one way or another. According to the law of cause and effect or the law of *karma*, every action has a reaction.

Good actions result in inner peace of mind whereas bad actions disturb the mental peace. A bad person may appear to enjoy outer wealth while suffering inwardly because of wrong actions. Conversely, a good person may seem to suffer outwardly while enjoying inner peace of mind because of good actions performed.

All physical and mental forces in Nature obey the universal law of cause and effect. Explaining the law of cause and effect, **Sivananda** (1887–1963), the great spiritual master of the 20th century, wrote: "The laws of gravitation, cohesion, adhesion, attraction and repulsion, the law of like and dislike on the physical plane, the laws of relativity and contiguity, the law of association on the mental plane, all operate in strict accordance with this law of cause and effect. From the vibration of an electron to the revolution of a mighty planet, from the falling of a mango to the ground to the powerful willing of a Yogi, from the motion of a runner in athletics to the movement of radio waves in the subtle ether, from the transmitting of a telegraphic message to the telepathic communication of a Yogi in the thought-world—every event is the effect of some invisible force that works in happy concord and harmony with the law of cause and effect."[5]

Whether the law of cause and effect applies universally is not a question of belief. **Yogananda**, in his famous book *Autobiography of a Yogi,* observed: "The law of gravitation worked as efficiently before Newton as after him. The cosmos would be fairly chaotic if its laws could not operate without the sanction of human belief."[6]

Those who do not understand this logical law of cause and effect as the law of justice usually accuse God of being unjust, wrong, and tyrannical. Some people complain, if God loves everyone, why does God allow suffering? This complaint is unreasonable. People often cause suffering to themselves by their own wrongdoing. For instance, if a person eats too much food and then suffers an upset stomach, can the server of the food ever be blamed? God has bestowed intellect upon people to discriminate between right and wrong. If people, out of egoism or ignorance, perform wrong actions, they reap the fruits of their own wrong actions. God is always just, reasonable, and fair. God makes no errors!

It is in accordance with the law of cause and effect that people create their destiny with their actions. People are free to choose their actions, but once an action is taken, its consequence is bound to follow. Just as our freely chosen actions in the past have created our present, our freely chosen actions in the present will create our future.

5. The Mystery of Death

Continuity is evident everywhere in Nature — day follows night, summer follows winter, and the full moon follows the new moon. A seed creates a tree, which in turn creates a seed. A father procreates a son, and the son, in turn, becomes a father. Similarly, birth is followed by death, and death is followed by birth. Upon death, only a physical form is destroyed. The life principle itself does not die. According to modern science, the essence called energy is indestructible. Therefore, the transmigration of soul or reincarnation, which implies a series of births and deaths, is both rational and scientific.

Just as sleep is an intermediate state between two waking states, death is an intermediate state between two births. Describing the mystery of death, life after death, and reincarnation, **Sivananda** wrote: "This subtle body comes out with all its impressions and tendencies at the time of death of the gross physical body. It is like vapor. It cannot be seen by the physical eye. It is the subtle body that goes to heaven. It manifests again in a gross form. This re-manifestation of the subtle form into the gross physical form is called reincarnation. You may deny this law, but it exists. It is inexorable and unrelenting."[7]

People who do not believe in life after death often believe in ghosts. To become a ghost, the soul must be able to survive a physical death; otherwise, who becomes the ghost? **Satyananda** (1923–2002), one of the greatest spiritual masters of India, observed: "In recent research on dying, the experiences of those who have been revived after death have been recorded. It was found that they first entered into darkness and then felt agony and pain. They heard peculiar cries and screaming. After some time they found the darkness was diminishing and the light was growing little by little, just like a dawn of a new day....Then they returned again through the same darkness. Now, it is not the experience that is important here, but who experienced it. If a man was dead and nothing survived, how could he have this experience? This proves that the soul survives death."[8]

In his famous book *Play of Consciousness*, **Muktananda** reveals the cycle of birth and rebirth in these words: "The blue star in which I had traveled is found in the *sahasrara* [The top-most spiritual center in the crown of the head] of every creature. Its brilliance can vary, but its size is the same. And it is by means of this star that the individual soul passes from one body to another in the cycle of birth and rebirth. However many times a man is burned or buried, the blue star will always stay the same. It leaves the body at death, but stays at the place of death for eleven days. Afterwards, according to destiny, it carries the soul with its sins and virtues to different worlds. The blue star is the self-propelled vehicle of the individual soul. When the individual is born again, the blue star is born with it."[9]

Heredity alone cannot logically explain the difference

in the inherent qualities of individuals. The doctrine of reincarnation or rebirth provides a satisfactory explanation, for instance, in the inequalities of babies born into the same family. **Yogananda** observed: "According to the law of cause and effect, every action creates a commensurate reaction. Therefore, whatever is happening to us now must be a result of something we have done previously. If there is nothing in this life to account for present circumstances, the inescapable conclusion is that the cause was set in motion at some prior time; that is, in some past human existence."[10]

Evolution through rebirth is a law of Nature. It is a necessity for evolution. Actually, death is just an exit, a point where the evolution of a person's mind enters into another phase. **Vishnu Tirtha** (1895–1969) wrote: "Thus a man goes on developing his faculties from birth to birth in his march towards the final goal of perfection. The phenomenon of transmigration of soul is thus a natural, simple, and reasonable one, sufficient to explain the many intricate problems of human psychology otherwise not explainable by western psychologists, such as instinct, sub-consciousness, differences in intellectual capacities of different persons, manifestations of unusually abnormally advanced powers of mind and intellect in certain children without their having received any previous training and similar other spontaneous phenomena usually met with."[11]

It is said that the thought that occupies the mind of a dying person at the moment of death determines the nature of the next birth. At the time of death only that thought, good or bad, comes to the mind, which was predominant during the whole lifetime. It would be difficult for people who have been thinking evil thoughts throughout their lifetime to have good thoughts at the time of their death.

6. Does Life Begin with Birth?

The word "birth" relates to the physical body. If one birth is possible, why not a whole succession of births? The transmigration of soul implies a series of births and deaths. Modern science has not yet been able to unravel the secret of soul.

Of the doctrine of rebirth, **Carl G. Jung** (1875–1961), the famous Swiss-born analytical psychologist, wrote: "I could well imagine that I might have lived in former centuries and there encountered questions I was not yet able to answer; that I had to be born again because I had not fulfilled the task that was given to me."[12]

Reincarnation is once again attracting the intellectuals in the West. Speaking about reincarnation, **Vivekananda** (1863–1902), a great spiritual master of India, said: "Hinduism and Buddhism have it for their foundation; the educated classes among the ancient Egyptians believed in it; the ancient Persians arrived at it; some of the Greek philosophers made it the corner-stone of their philosophy; the Parsis among the Hebrews accepted it; and the Sufis, among the Mohammedans, almost universally acknowledged its truth."[13]

About the acceptance of reincarnation in early Christianity, **Yogananda** wrote: "The early Christian church accepted the doctrine of reincarnation, which was expounded by the Gnostics and by numerous church fathers, including Clement of Alexandria, the celebrated Origen (both 3rd Century), and St. Jerome (5th Century)."[14] The Bible mentions that John the Baptist is Elias. According to **Yogananda**'s book[15], when **Jesus** said, Elias is come already, he meant that the soul of the prophet Elias had reincarnated in the body of John the Baptist. Referring to John the Baptist, **Jesus** said, "If ye will receive it, this is Elias, which for to come." (Matthew 11:14.) "But I say unto you, that Elias is come already, and they knew him not, but have done unto him whatsoever they listed. Likewise shall also the Son of man suffer of them. Then the disciples understood that he spake unto them of John the Baptist." (Matthew 17:12-13).

Commenting on the belief of current Christianity, **Sivananda** wrote: "Christians believe that one life determines and settles everything. How could this be? How can the everlasting future of man be made to depend on one small insignificant life? If in this life he believes in Christ, he will get eternal peace in heaven; if he is unbeliever in the present life, he will get eternal damnation. He will be thrown forever in the lake of fire or into a horrible hell. Is this not the most irrational doctrine? Should he not get his chances for correction and improvement? The doctrine of reincarnation is quite rational. It gives ample chances for man's growth, rectification, and gradual evolution."[16] **Sivananda** further stated: "If we deny pre-existence and rebirth and take into consideration that life begins with this birth only and ends completely with the death of the body and there is nothing more, then it will be no compensation for the virtuous man who has done noble actions and for the wicked man who has done crimes. The chain of cause and effect, antecedent and consequence, will be broken abruptly. There will be terrible injustice everywhere."[17]

The very understanding of reincarnation not only brings hope to people who have lost all hope, but also deters them from performing harmful acts. Encouraging people to perform good actions, **Yogananda** wrote: "Your present poverty or opulence, disease or health, is brought about by your own past actions; and your present life and action will determine your future."[18]

It is never too late to mend. Sow the seed now and it will grow in its season. Whether Hindus or Buddhists, Christians or Zoroastrians, Muslims or Jews, people can certainly improve by purifying their minds of anger, jealousy, hatred, greed, lust, selfishness, and prejudice. A good understanding of the doctrine of rebirth will help pave the way for a noble world to emerge.

7. Religious Fanaticism Incites Terrorism

There is nothing that has deluged the world with more horror than religious fanaticism. While the name of God is meant to promote love and peace, it is frequently the cause of bloodshed, hatred, and cruelty. **Kofi A. Annan** (1938–present), the seventh Secretary-General of the United Nations, said: "Each of us has the right to take pride in our particular faith or heritage. But the notion that what is ours is necessarily in conflict with what is theirs is both false and dangerous. It has resulted in endless enmity and conflict, leading men to commit the greatest of crimes in the name of a higher power."[19]

The Jews believe in the Torah, Christians in the Bible, Muslims in the Koran, Hindus in the Bhagavad Gita, and Sikhs in the Guru Granth Sahib. These holy books reiterate that there is but one God pervading everything, animate and inanimate. Holy books do not teach or justify the exploitation or murder of innocent people for pleasure, selfishness, or comfort. The Christian, the Jew, the Muslim, the Sikh, the Hindu, and the Buddhist commandments are all the same, such as, do not kill, do not steal, do not hate, and do not lie. In fact, these commandments encourage people to purify their mind. It is a sad fact that some people have twisted and distorted the interpretations of holy books for their own selfish motives. This is the root cause of religious fanaticism, hatred, and war.

Misled by perverted interpretations, the blind followers of a particular religion sometimes commit violent acts. These fanatics and dogmatists are ready to kill or to be killed for their so-called religious ideas. Thus, their belief of being religious hides their irreligious crimes. **Sivananda**, in his article *The Unity That Underlies All Religions*, wrote: "All systems of religion are equally divine and true. The conflicting points are all due to misconception and misconstruction of truths on account of prejudice, bigotry, lack of purity of heart, and subtlety and purity of intellect, and perverted condition of the intellect of people."

Ordinary minds often fail to grasp the mystical tenets of these sacred books. God is limitless and, as such, His knowledge is unlimited. In fact, the Infinite Reality cannot be expressed by the gross finite words of any language in the world. It is wrong to think that limitless knowledge can be sealed in a single book, which is finite. **Vivekananda** aptly remarked: "Was there ever a more horrible blasphemy than the statement that all the knowledge of God is confined to this or that book? How dare men call God infinite and yet try to compress Him within the covers of a little book!"[20]

8. How to Respond to the Threat of Violence

The greatest threat to world peace is savage fanaticism that takes the form of violence, tyranny, or terrorism. **Ramakrishna** (1836–1886), one of the foremost saints of India, was once asked: "Sir, if a wicked man is about to do harm, or actually does so, should we keep quiet then?"

Ramakrishna replied: "A man living in society should make a show of *tamas*[f] to protect himself from evil-minded people. But he should not harm anybody in anticipation of harm likely to be done him."

Then, the master continued to tell the story of a snake and a saint who had asked the snake not to bite but did not forbid it to hiss. "So you must hiss at wicked people. You must frighten them lest they should do you harm. But never inject your venom into them."[21]

It is wrong to suppose that spiritual conduct is nonviolent in all cases. What may appear to be violent or cruel-heartedness in a certain situation could be a form of compassion if it stops wickedness or wrong habits. Punishment, with no feeling of hatred or revenge, could bring about reformation. For example, a father might punish his unruly son with an outward show of anger, while maintaining an inward feeling of love for his son's reformation. In the matter of violence, **Rama Tirtha** advised: "Therefore it is but natural for you to do your bounden duty, with all your might, even to take up

---

[f]*Tamas* is one of three *gunas* (attributes) in Nature — *sattva* (purity), *rajas* (action), and *tamas* (inertia). Anger is a typical characteristic of *tamas*.

arms, if necessary, to be defensively offensive in the interest of self-preservation and to safeguard your own or your national freedom and cultural heritage, based on Truth."[22]

Justifying Arjuna's fighting in the Mahabharata War of 3139 BC, **Sivananda** said: "But the battle fought by Arjuna was not an exhibition of cruelty, but an execution of one's own duty. The war fell to his lot as pure duty or *Svadharma*. Arjuna did not want it himself. He did not impose it on the Kauravas. He was challenged to it by them. He had to defend himself and his clan. As a Kshatriya, it was his sacred duty and moral responsibility to fight for the defense of his rights. Thus, Arjuna's fighting the battle being purely duty-bound, is thoroughly justified."[23]

All our actions, however, must be directed with reason and compassion depending upon time, place, and situation. **Rama Tirtha**, when asked whether to kill the tyrant even before he actually commits the tyranny, replied: "Rama does not agree with this saying, 'Kill the criminal even before he commits any crime.' It is unjust to punish a man on mere suspicion."[24]

9. War Breeds War

The common response to terrorism so far has been to retaliate with violence. Since any act has a motive behind it, it is wise to question the motive before retaliating. Advising how to resolve conflicts, **Yogananda** stated: "The first line of action should be to use all spiritual and moral power possible to counter evil; and to strive to change the world's inclination to war and violence by removing the causes that strengthen evil — poverty and hunger, disease, injustice, greed, and selfish interests."[25]

Remember, enmity often escalates when violence is returned. Likewise, a war, no matter how victorious, often leaves behind a spirit of revenge in the defeated people. This, then, becomes the cause of continual wars, from generation to generation.

The negative vibrations created by wars disturb the balance of Nature. This results in epidemics, droughts, floods, storms, and earthquakes. **Yogananda** noted: "The agonies of the people who died in the world war created the subtle cause of the epidemic of Spanish influenza, which immediately followed the war, and killed 20 million people while the war itself killed about 10 million only."[26]

Fundamentally, the very concept of war as a permanent solution is a grave mistake. India's history proves that violent fighting for many centuries never succeeded in winning India's independence, whereas only 25 years of nonviolent fighting under the able leadership of Mahatma Gandhi against the British rule was successful. The sooner people realize the power of nonviolence, the better off humanity will be. **Yogananda** stated: "Gandhi's doctrine of resisting evil by the force of love has already proven to be practical. In this machine age when man's destructive power has grown to far exceed his powers of construction, Gandhi has given a universal panacea for the ills of our social system. To conquer all social and political evils, we must use the most formidable spiritual weapon, namely, 'resistance by love.' War breeds war, and it can be prevented only by non-cooperation and the overcoming power of love."[27]

Human history reveals that many ill-informed political leaders have pushed people and nations into wars. Every war is an act of terror — thousands of people are killed, thousands of women become widows, and thousands of children become orphans. The future of humanity needs a permanent respite from killing. Between 1933 and 1945, Nazis led by Adolf Hitler (1889–1945), an Austrian-born German dictator, murdered over 20 million people (including some six million Jewish civilians in Europe during the Holocaust). Soviet dictators Vladimir Lenin (1870–1924) and Josef Stalin (1879–1953) were responsible for murdering about 43 million people. During the Second World War[28] (1939–1945), the U.S. dropped atomic bombs[29] on the Japanese cities of Hiroshima (August 6, 1945) and Nagasaki (August 9, 1945) killing about 120,000 civilians.

The ruthlessness of the September 11, 2001, terrorist attacks against the United States killed more than 3,000 innocent people. And on it goes, endlessly.

10. Conquer Evil with Good

World history proves that any nation that ruthlessly rules or exploits weaker nations is bound to lose its influence eventually. There have been times when the world trembled with horror — those were the periods when the powerful empires of Greece, Rome, and Persia forcibly conquered their neighbors. Once, Mogul invaders were seen as terrorists to their neighboring countries. Before the Second World War, the British Empire was so far-reaching that it was said, "The sun never set upon the British Empire." Many mighty kingdoms, which at one time struck terror into the world, have now lost their positions of supremacy.

The law of survival of the fittest, which is the law of the jungle, need no longer govern relationships among nations. "An eye for an eye" and "a tooth for a tooth" are doctrines based on reactionary or animal-like nature. But, man is more than an animal. Animals live by instinct whereas human beings have intellect and intuition. The image of Jesus upon the cross remains a supreme example of the doctrine based on divine nature: return good for evil. It is said that the last words **Jesus** spoke on the cross were: "Father, forgive them; for they know not what they do." (Luke 23:34)

People and nations can prove their greatness through their broadminded and unselfish actions, and by showing greater love toward others, not greater hatred. All civilized persons and nations would do well to follow the divine principles of tolerance and expansiveness.

Since the news media play a tremendous role in influencing public opinion, televised talks on spirituality would go a long way in promoting fairness and justice in the world. It is true that some people or nations commit evil more than others, but those who are good are challenged to conquer evil, not create it. For instance, killing is a perpetration of evil. **Satyananda** remarked: "Only He who has given life can take life. A man has no right to take the life of another man. No Government has the right to execute anyone anymore. Nobody has the right to kill another, except God and nature."[30]

11. How to Stop Terrorism

Can a "war on terrorism" that exposed a global network of terrorist organizations be won by attacking the nations suspected of harboring perpetrators? Terrorism is committed by individuals and organizations, not by whole countries. Attacking countries to find terrorists is like looking for a needle by burning the haystack.

If we are serious about stopping terrorism, we must get rid of selfish interests and greed at individual, commercial, and political levels. If the majority of the world population remains illiterate, hungry, and poor, there will be a continual rise in terrorism, and the prosperous will remain insecure. Even the most advanced nations will not be able to sustain their progress unless underdeveloped nations are also elevated.

Martin Luther King, Jr. (1929–1968), an American Baptist minister who was honored with the Nobel Prize for Peace in 1964, said: "A nation that continues year after year to spend more money on military defense than on programs of social uplift is approaching spiritual doom." Money must be used for construction, not for destruction. Worldwide military expenditure surged during 2003, reaching $956 billion, of which the United States accounted for 47 percent. Between fiscal year 2001 and 2004, military expenditure surged from $354 billion to $547 billion in the USA The USA remains the top military spender in the world, while the next four are Japan, Britain, France, and China. Recommending better use of money, **Yogananda** wrote: "Because of ambitious and evil politicians, the earth has suffered two world wars, and faces the prospect of a third world conflict. If the money spent on destruction were instead collected in an international fund, it could remove the slums of the world, eradicate hunger, and greatly advance medical science, giving every man, woman, and child a better chance to live in the peace of a God-centered life."[31]

The United Nations (UN) is unique among international organizations that administer international funding to provide humanitarian assistance. Its various agencies and programs are oriented toward building a world of greater peace, prosperity, stability, and justice. While awarding the 2001 Nobel Prize for Peace jointly to the UN and its Secretary-General, **Kofi A. Annan**, the Norwegian Committee rightfully stated that "the only negotiable route to global peace and cooperation goes by way of the United Nations."

On October 24, 1945, at the end of the Second World War, the UN was created to maintain international peace and security, to develop friendly relations among nations, to cooperate in solving international economic, social, cultural and humanitarian problems, to promote respect for human rights and fundamental freedoms, and to be a center for harmonizing the actions of nations in attaining these ends.

The UN is divided into six principal structures: the General Assembly, the Security Council, the Economic and Social Council, the Trusteeship Council, the International Court of Justice, and the Secretariat. The Security Council is responsible for peace and security in the world. The International Court of Justice is the principal judicial organ of the UN. Its seat is at the Peace Palace in The Hague (Netherlands).

Political power that lacks respect for human rights is very dangerous. The protection of basic human rights and human worth is paramount to spirituality. On December 10, 1948, the General Assembly of the UN created a turning point in the history of human rights by unanimously adopting the Universal Declaration of Human Rights (see Appendix B). The declaration contains 30 articles, which clearly state the civil, political, economic, social, and cultural rights that all human beings in every country should enjoy.

The UN decisively demonstrated its authority when, on November 29, 1990, its Security Council authorized the use of "all necessary means" to expel the invading country Iraq from Kuwait. In order to protect smaller nations, an almighty UN is necessary. It is vital that all member nations strive toward making the UN more powerful than ever before. Any nation that invades another without consent of the UN Security Council risks violation of the UN Charter.

Today, the UN concentrates on four areas: the preservation of peace, humanitarian assistance, economic and social development, and human rights. Since its inception, the UN has grown enormously, bringing 191 countries—all the independent countries of our earth—into a semblance of unity. However, fair treatment among member nations is still lacking. On the world stage, the UN is unable at times to prevent invasions and destruction. While our world is certainly better than before, the UN is yet to be capable of **replacing "Might is right" with "Right is might."**

The UN will function successfully only if its member nations have noble leaders infused with the spirit of tolerance, cooperation, and friendship. **Herman Hesse** (1877–1962), the German writer and winner of Nobel Prize for Literature in 1946, said: "The greatest threat to our world and its peace comes from those who want war, who prepare for it, and who, by holding out vague promises of future peace or by instilling fear of foreign aggression, try to make us accomplices to their plans." In this world of increased globalization and economic interdependence, political leaders need to act with universal vision—not narrow motives. Otherwise, the UN will fail, like the League of Nations failed after the First World War because of its inability to prevent aggression by Germany, Italy, and Japan in the 1930s.

Nuclear weapons and their proliferation still remain a major threat to international peace and security. No plan for giving control of nuclear weapons to the UN has yet succeeded.

Even though more than a hundred nations have become members since the creation of the UN in 1945, the UN's Security Council is still dominated by the same five permanent members — Russia, China, France, the United Kingdom, and the United States. **These five permanent members retain veto powers that can be used to protect their own interests.** It is noteworthy that the European Union (EU) has succeeded in preventing wars among its members. Following the EU model, the UN can facilitate the formation of five regional unions of nations throughout the world to help win the "war on terrorism." Once all the regional unions of neighboring nations are developed, their representation could eventually raise the United Nations' status to that of a "world government." This way, the UN's decisions will reflect the interests of a larger community of nations.

12. The Root of Crime and War

The root of crime and war is in the human mind. Therefore, the most effective way to stop terrorism, violence, oppression, hatred, deception, hypocrisy, and corruption is to improve the quality of the human mind. Without a change in the character of individuals, the war on terrorism cannot be won. Wrong is often committed under the influence of ignorance or delusion. A wrongdoing must be condemned, but the wrongdoer is more to be pitied than condemned.

Even a criminal can be transformed into a noble person by killing the germ of the disease — ignorance. For example, Valmiki, the author of the famous Indian epic *Ramayana*, had been the bandit Ratnakar before he was transformed into a great sage. Mary Magdalene became virtuous in the company of Jesus Christ. It is said that she was about to be stoned to death when Jesus saved her life by saying, "Let he amongst you who is without sin cast the first stone." (John 8:7) Angulimala was a ferocious robber, but he became saintly with Buddha. We need not condemn anyone, because those who are criminals today can evolve higher tomorrow. If we condemn those who are fallen or backward, they will never be able to rise. Therefore, we should treat the aggressive, unreasonable, and hostile wrongdoers in the manner that doctors attend to their patients.

If bad people cannot stop doing bad, why should good people stop doing good? Darkness is never removed by imposing a thicker darkness. To dispel darkness, we need to bring in light. **Anger, greed, jealousy, hatred, and egoism are enemies of peace.** In order to decrease evil or violence, the number of people evolving spiritually must increase. The 14th **Dalai Lama, Tenzin Gyatso** (1935–present), said: "The calamity of 9/11 demonstrated that modern technology and human intelligence guided by hatred can lead to immense destruction. Such terrible acts are a violent symptom of an afflicted mental state. To respond wisely and effectively, we need to be guided by more healthy states of mind, not just to avoid feeding the flames of hatred, but to respond skillfully. We would do well to remember that the war against hatred and terror can be waged on this, the internal front, too."[32]

Pointing out that threats and punishments never prevent crime, **Rama Tirtha** wrote: "Precepts, binding principles, artificial rules of conduct and unnatural morality will never cure matters. Remember that. 'Thou shalt not do this' and 'Thou shalt do that' will never bring about any reform. If these rules and these wise counsels could mend matters, the promised Kingdom of God would have been established long ago, the world would have been a heaven and not the kind of a world it is today. These will not cure matters. Your punishment, your jails and prisons will not improve matters. The world will have to realize, whether today or tomorrow, that it is a great blunder to believe in the efficacy or virtue of jails and prison-houses. Threats and punishments never prevented sin. In order to mend matters effectually, you will have to instill knowledge, culture, living knowledge, that is what is necessary.... Instead of keeping jails and prisons, you will have to teach the criminals, instruct them and acquaint them with the divine laws that govern the world."[33]

13. Yoga Transforms Human Behavior

The physical and psychological practices of yoga purify the human mind. Since yoga treats the mind, it brings about a significant and rapid change in both the character and behavior of an individual who sincerely practices it. **Satyananda** observed: "So if you turn back the pages of the history books and try to find an answer as to why man kills man, the only intelligent explanation that will come to your mind is that man has not been able to effect a change in his inner nature. And the reason why he hasn't been able to do this is simply because he has not known how."[34]

Just as butter is manifested when milk is churned, the divinity that is latent within a human being is manifested when yoga is practiced. There is a textbook on yoga called *Yoga Sutras* written by the renowned sage Patanjali who is considered the foremost authority on yoga. His ideas about the human mind, expressed in 196 precise verses in *Yoga Sutras*, are more advanced than the modern theories of psychology.

The word "psychology" is derived from the Greek word *psukhe*, which means soul. In the West, **Socrates** (469 BC–399 BC), the Greek philosopher of great fame, talked about the soul and its immortality. By exploring and adapting the techniques of Patanjali's *Yoga Sutras*, the field of psychology could greatly assist human evolution. The goal is the highest possible evolution of the human race. From this perspective, the future belongs to the *Yoga Sutras* because its approach is scientific, and not belief oriented. It can be predicted that any religion that cannot raise itself to Patanjali's scientific level may have trouble surviving in the future.

Laying down the eight systematic steps of yoga, described at length in chapter three, Patanjali revealed superb techniques for concentrating the human mind. According to his *Yoga Sutras*, the greater the duration of inner concentration, progressively termed *Dharana* (concentration), *dhyan* (meditation), and *Samadhi* (absorption), the more qualities, capacities, and changes take place in a human being.

Changes are effected not by changing others, but by changing oneself. Individuals make a family, families make a society, societies make a nation, and nations make a world. Thus, individuals *are* the world. When individuals change, the world changes. There is no other way. The Siddha Yoga master **Chidvilasananda** (1955–present), remarked: "Where is the world? Where is it? It's you and I. If there is no peace within you, how can there be peace in the world? We must experience peace within ourselves."[35]

14. Global Harmony

Times are changing rapidly and we must adjust accordingly. Currently, the world is passing through a period of crisis, nevertheless everything is still evolving. It is humanism, not nationalism or militarism, that can ultimately bring peace and prosperity in the world. Every human being belongs to a single human race. Just as the different organs of a human body help one another in a natural way, so can we, as members of one global family, share our resources. In the words of **Rama Tirtha**: "The hand is always ready to help all the other parts of the body. When our feet are in pain or any other part is hurt, our hand immediately comes to relieve us of our pain, without at all thinking that the feet are lower than the hand or that the mouth, nose, ears, or eyes may contain impurities. Similarly, we should never look down upon others."[36]

The current trend is inevitably toward continental and global harmony. The phenomenal growth of the Internet, speedy air travel, and wireless communication technology has brought people of different religions, regions, and languages so close together that the whole world is now a closely-knit unit. Different nations are now interdependent with diplomatic and economic relationships. What once may have been considered an internal dispute of a nation now potentially affects the whole world, just as a diseased knee-joint affects the other parts of the physical body.

In the future, national boundaries are expected to become less and less significant as more and more people interact through modern computer technology. The day is not far off when the people and nations of the world will unite. **Yogananda** declared: "We must learn that it can no longer be Asia for Asiatics, Europe for Europeans, America for Americans, and so on, but a United States of the World under God, in which each human being can be an ideal citizen of the globe with every opportunity for fulfillment in body, mind, and soul."[37]

Global harmony can be achieved by overcoming our shortsightedness. **Jawaharlal Nehru** (1889–1964), a world-renowned Indian statesman, observed: "For a long time Europeans imagined that ancient history meant only the history of Greece and of Rome and of the Jews. All the rest of the world apparently was a wilderness in those days, according to their old way of thinking. Later they discovered how limited was their knowledge, when their own scholars and archaeologists told them of China and India and other countries."[38]

There is a fable of a frog that lived in a well, which illustrates how limited the vision of individuals, nations, and religions can be. According to the fable, one day, a frog that lived in a lake happened to fall into a well where a well-frog lived. When the lake-frog mentioned that his lake was a lot bigger than the well, the well-frog heartily laughed at him in disbelief.

In the modern age, when small minds often dominate world events, humanity is at a great risk of self-destruction through the use of nuclear, chemical, and biological weapons. What is the use of our scientific progress if the human mind is not at peace? This peace can be gained through meditation on the innermost soul. Once this meditation is experienced, love naturally wells up in the heart. This love arising out of meditation is the way to overcome jealousy, hatred, prejudice, and hostility in the world. Meditation on a world-wide scale can win the "war on terrorism." Indeed, meditation, not the power of technology, money, or weapons, is the way to save the world. The power of spirituality is even greater than the power of an atom bomb.

Chapter 2

A Call for Harmony among Nations

Yogananda Paramahansa (1893–1952)

CHAPTER 2
A Call for Harmony among Nations

It is dangerous to live in a world filled with conflicts, terrorism, and threats of warfare. Until spirituality is applied to the practical world, modern scientific technology is likely to be misused. **Yogananda,** one of the greatest spiritual masters of India, declared: "Wars are bound to go on until the United States of Europe and the United States of Asia are evolved, to prepare the way for the United States of the World, with God guiding all nations."[39]

While leaders of most countries concentrate on strengthening their alliances with major world powers, few consider the benefits of unification with neighboring nations. The European Union has demonstrated that increased coordination among neighboring nations can be achieved while still preserving their national identities. Unlike the United States, the European Union is founded on international treaties among sovereign countries, rather than on a single constitution. The European Union has proved successful so far in preventing armed conflicts and in promoting peace and economic prosperity among its member nations. Regions such as South Asia, the Middle East, South America, and Africa can gain peace, stability, security, and economic prosperity by following the concept of the European Union.

In South Asia, where both India and Pakistan possess nuclear weapons, any nuclear disaster would potentially affect the whole world. The 14th **Dalai Lama, Tenzin Gyatso**, the spiritual leader[g] of the Tibetan people, said: "Today, we are truly a global family. What happens in one part of the world may affect us all. This, of course, is not only true of the negative things that happen, but is equally valid for the positive developments. We not only know what happens elsewhere, thanks to extraordinary modern communications technology, we are also directly affected by events that occur far away. We feel a sense of sadness when children are starving in Eastern Africa. Similarly, we feel a sense of joy when a family is reunited after decades of separation by the Berlin Wall. Our crops and livestock are contaminated, and our health and livelihood threatened when a nuclear accident happens miles away in another country. Our own security is enhanced when peace breaks out between warring parties in other continents."[40]

1. From Colonialism to the Cold War

Throughout history, powerful nations have used "divide and conquer" tactics to increase their own economic and military superiority.

After the discovery of America on October 12, 1492, by the Italian explorer **Christopher Columbus** (1451-1506), the British gradually established 13 large colonies in America during the years 1607 to 1733. On July 4, 1776, the Continental Congress adopted the "Declaration of Independence," thereby freeing these 13 colonies from the British rule to found the United States of America.

During the reign of **Queen Victoria** (1837-1901), Britain became the world's wealthiest empire by establishing colonies or "overseas territories" in Australia, Canada, South Africa, Egypt, and India. Weakened by the Great Depression of 1929, the British Empire began to shrink. By 1931, Australia, New Zealand, and Canada had become independent. After the end of the Second World War (1939-1945), when "the winds of change" blew through South Asia, Africa, and islands in the Pacific and Indian Oceans, most of the remaining colonies of the British Empire became independent. Thus, the British Empire was reduced to its original European homeland.

European colonial dominance over the non-European

---

[g]Tibetan Buddhists believe that each Dalai Lama is a reincarnation of his predecessor, who is considered an incarnation of the Bodhisattva Avalokitesvara.

world virtually ended when the weakened British were forced to abandon India, "the brightest jewel in the English Crown." Before leaving on August 14, 1947, after ruling India for 190 years, the British partitioned India into two countries: India with a Hindu majority and Pakistan with a Muslim majority. The rationale for creating Pakistan was the notion that Hindus and Muslims could not coexist. Muslims and Hindus, who had been living side by side in friendship for centuries, were forced apart without any cultural necessity. In the wake of the Partition, some 12 million Hindus and Muslims crossed the India-Pakistan borders. This mass migration led to communal massacres, killing more than 200,000 people.

At the time the British divided the Indian subcontinent, Pakistan consisted of two regions — the northwest region was named West Pakistan and the eastern region was named East Pakistan — separated by 1,100 miles of territory within India. The rest of British India officially became the Republic of India. The notion that the common Muslim religion would hold East Pakistan and West Pakistan together fell apart when East Pakistan broke away in 1971 and became the independent nation of Bangladesh.

Since the names of Pakistan and Bangladesh bear no reference to the country from which they originated from, it is often unclear to newer generations that both Pakistan and Bangladesh were once an integral part of India. Although other countries such as Korea, Germany, and Vietnam were also divided, they retained the name of their country of origin, a key element of their heritage.

After the end of the Second World War on October 24, 1945, the two superpowers, the USA and USSR, representing two different political and economic systems, confronted each other in an unfriendly relationship known as the Cold War. In 1945, Korea was split into two countries: North Korea under Soviet control and South Korea under American control. In 1949, Germany was split into two countries: East Germany under Soviet control and West Germany under the control of

Britain, France, and the USA. The control of the city of Berlin was divided between East Germany and West Germany by constructing a wall between the two parts of the city. In 1954, Vietnam was split into two countries: North Vietnam supported by the USSR and South Vietnam supported by the USA. Thus divided, these countries became a focal point for the notorious Cold War tension.

2. From the Cold War to the European Union

The Berlin Wall, which separated East and West Berlin for 28 years, finally tumbled down on November 9, 1989. The fall of the Wall will always be remembered as the primary symbol of the end of the Cold War and the collapse of Communism in Eastern Europe and the former Soviet Union. The official reunion of Germany on October 3, 1990, was not only one of the most celebrated events in world history, but it also inspired the world toward mutual understanding, friendship, and peace.

On November 1, 1993, the European Community, established in 1967, became the European Union (EU) as the Maastricht Treaty took effect. The EU is an alliance of democratic European countries that agree to work together for peace and prosperity. On January 11, 1999, the Euro was introduced as a common European currency, enabling people, services, capital, and goods to move freely among the participating countries. Between 1999 and 2001, the twelve EU countries—Belgium, Germany, France, Italy, Luxembourg, the Netherlands, Ireland, Greece, Spain, Portugal, Austria, and Finland—kept their old national currencies in circulation while introducing the new euro. Effective January 1, 2002, these countries gave up their old currencies forever to make the Euro as their only currency of legal tender. However, Denmark, Sweden, and the United Kingdom (and the ten nations that joined the EU on May 1, 2004) do not currently participate in the euro. The introduction of the Euro is the most successful effort in uniting EU countries economically. Moreover, the Euro has now established itself as a strong currency in the international money markets.

The integration of European countries began with just six nations — Belgium, Germany, France, Italy, Luxembourg, and the Netherlands — in 1952. Denmark, Ireland and the United Kingdom joined the integration in 1973, Greece in 1981, Spain and Portugal in 1986, Austria, Finland, and Sweden in 1995. On May 1, 2004, as many as ten more nations — Cyprus, the Czech Republic, Estonia, Hungary, Latvia, Lithuania, Malta, Poland, Slovakia, and Slovenia — joined the EU, enlarging it to twenty-five member countries (EU25). These countries have joined the EU to ensure their peace, prosperity, security, and stability. After successfully growing from 6 to 25 member nations, the European Union is now preparing for the next enlargement, perhaps one day developing into a "United States of Europe."

The EU, headquartered in Brussels, Belgium, covers most of the territories of ancient Rome. It is governed by five main institutions: the European Commission, the European Parliament, the Council of the European Union, the European Court of Justice, and the Court of Auditors. The European Central Bank (ECB), one of the additional five bodies of the EU, manages the Euro currency.

The European Parliament members are directly elected by the citizens of all member countries. The new EU25 Parliament for the 2004–2009 term comprises 732 representatives. Interestingly, the seating arrangement in the European Parliament is by party allegiance and not by nationality. Today, the European Union has, as one of its greatest assets, the cultural and linguistic diversity of the European nations. The EU promotes unity while preserving diversity. It is noteworthy that the EU has eliminated the death penalty within its member nations. People in the EU hold a common European passport. They have freedom to live, work, and study in any of the member nations. All EU countries are committed to peace, democracy, the rule of law, and respect for human rights. The combined resources of all

Mahatma Gandhi (1869–1948)

EU countries constitute the second greatest concentration of industrial power in the world.

3. Gandhi Opposed Partition Based on Religion

Like Europe, the region of South Asia, known as the Indian subcontinent, could immensely benefit from the European Union model. The European Union is a political, economic, and social model that mainly inspires peace. It has set a practical precedent for gradual development toward the unification of neighboring nations. The Indian subcontinent is known for diverse cultures, languages, and religions. In ancient times, it was a unified and prosperous entity. Using "divide and conquer" tactics, invaders succeeded in weakening the basic unity of the people. The downfall of the Indian subcontinent began the day division based on religion was introduced. To divide people simply on the basis of differences in religion is a grave and indefensible mistake. People should be known by their actions, not by their religions.

Mohandas K. Gandhi (1869–1948), known as Mahatma Gandhi, the most revered Indian leader, unified people and freed India from Great Britain using the same principles of love and nonviolence as had been taught by Lord Gautama Buddha and Lord Jesus Christ. In his name, "Mahatma" is a title meaning "great soul." Speaking about the nobility of Gandhi, **Albert Einstein** wrote: "A leader of his people, unsupported by only outward authority; a politician whose success rests not upon craft nor mastery of technical devices, but simply on the convincing power of his personality; a victorious fighter who has always scorned the use of force; a man of wisdom and humility, armed with resolve and inflexible consistency, who has devoted all his strength to the uplifting of his people and the betterment of their lot; a man who has confronted the brutality of Europe with the dignity of the simple human being, and thus at all times risen superior.

Generations to come, it may be, will scarce believe that such one as this ever in flesh and blood walked upon this earth."

Gandhi's doctrine of nonviolent protest to achieve political and social progress will live forever. Although Mahatma Gandhi was one of the greatest apostles of peace, it is a mystery that he was not awarded the famous Nobel Prize for Peace. The Nobel Prize for Peace is the only one of the six Nobel prizes that is not awarded by a Swedish committee. Alfred Nobel, the founder of the award, gave the task of selecting a recipient of the Nobel Prize for Peace to Norway. According to **Geir Lundestad**, Secretary of the Norwegian Nobel Committee since 1990: "Most observers will agree that the omission of Gandhi from the list of Nobel Laureates is a serious one, but it might be the only one of such a nature....Gandhi was, however, nominated five times, and he was put on the committee's short list three times. In 1948, the committee awarded no prize; it indicated that it had found 'no suitable living candidate,' a reference to Gandhi."

The India-Pakistan conflict in South Asia stems from the division of India in 1947. Believing that the Partition of the Indian subcontinent would lead to conflict between Pakistan and India, **Mahatma Gandhi** wrote to Lord Mountbatten, the Governor General of India: "It would be a blunder of first magnitude for the British to be party in any way whatsoever to the division of India."[41] **Gandhi** further stated in that letter, if the division had to come, it should take place only after the British had gone away.

After India's independence, in his speech at the Prayer Meeting on January 4, 1948, **Gandhi** said, "I shall, therefore, humbly say to the responsible leaders of Pakistan that though we are now two countries—which is a thing I never wanted—we should at least try to arrive at an agreement so that we could live as peaceful neighbors."

4. Solution to the Kashmir Issue

The relationship between India and Pakistan has been

strained since August 14, 1947, when Britain ceased its colonial rule in India. On June 1, 1947, the British Parliament passed the *Indian Independence Act of 1947*. Under this Act, the British not only divided the land into Pakistan and India, but also stipulated that the 562 princes of the various princely states could either remain independent or freely accede to India or Pakistan. By the time the British rule ended, Kashmir had not yet signed the Instrument of Accession to accede to either India or Pakistan. Technically, Kashmir became an independent nation on August 14, 1947 when the paramount power (sovereignty) of the British Crown over the princely states lapsed.

Although the majority of its population was Muslim, Kashmir was ruled by Hari Singh, a Hindu king. The term "Kashmir" refers to three distinct regions: the Valley of Kashmir, Jammu, and the region of Ladakh. Sufi Muslims, Hindu Brahmins, and Buddhists have lived together peacefully in Kashmir for generations. For the past 5,000 years, Kashmir has been a cradle of Kashmir Shaivism, a grand Hindu philosophy that has been kept alive by Kashmiri Brahmins called *Pandits*.

The modern history of Kashmir can be traced to the Treaty of Amritsar, signed on March 16, 1846. According to this Treaty, Gulab Singh, the Hindu king of Jammu, bought Kashmir for a sum of Rs. 7.5 million from the British Government. From 1846 to 1947, Gulab Singh, Ranbir Singh, Pratap Singh, and Hari Singh ruled Kashmir in succession.

On October 22, 1947, Pakistani forces disguised as local tribesmen launched a full-scale invasion of Kashmir. *Microsoft Encarta (2004)*, reports: "In October 1947, a rebellion broke out amid the Pashtun tribes in the western areas of Jammu and Kashmir. The Muslim Pashtuns had long resented the Hindu maharaja's rule, and in the wake of the British departure they moved to exploit the power vacuum and challenge the maharaja's authority. Pakistani irregular forces, comprising members of the Pakistani army disguised as local tribesmen, entered the fray to support the Pashtun rebels. Within a week the rebels and their allies attacked and seized the border town of Muzzafarabad and then moved toward Srinagar, the capital of Jammu and Kashmir. Hari Singh, now in a state of panic for fear Srinagar would fall to the rebels, appealed to Indian Prime Minister Jawaharlal Nehru for military assistance."

In his letter dated October 26, 1947, Hari Singh wrote to Lord Mountbatten, Britain's last Viceroy of India: "With the conditions obtaining at present in my State and the great emergency of the situation as it exists, I have no option but to ask for help from the Indian Dominion. Naturally they cannot send the help asked for by me without my State acceding to the Dominion of India. I have accordingly decided to do so and I attach the Instrument of Accession for acceptance by your Government."

On October 26, 1947, Hari Singh, the ruler of Jammu and Kashmir, willfully acceded to India by signing the Instrument of Accession. The Instrument of Accession was accepted by Lord Mountbatten on October 27, 1947, on behalf of the British Crown with the condition that the accession to India be ratified by the people of Kashmir when Kashmir's soil had been cleared of the invading Pakistanis. This condition was stated in Lord Mountbatten's official letter of acceptance dated October 27, 1947: "Consistently with their policy that in the case of any State where the issue of accession has been the subject of dispute, the question of accession should be decided in accordance with the wishes of the people of the State, it is my Government's wish that, as soon as law and order have been restored in Kashmir and her soil cleared of the invader, the question of the State's accession should be settled by a reference to the people."

After Kashmir's legal accession, Indian troops immediately entered Kashmir blocking further invasion, but not before invading Pakistan had occupied nearly one-third of Kashmir, which Pakistan holds to this day. Through the United Nations, a cease-fire agreement between Pakistan and

India was concluded on January 1, 1949.

China also occupies a portion of Kashmir. According to *Microsoft Encarta Online Encyclopedia 2004*, Kashmir covers a total area of 85,806 sq. miles. Chinese-controlled Kashmir has an area of about 16,500 sq. miles (19.2%); Pakistani-controlled Kashmir has an area of 30,476 sq. miles (35.5%). China and Pakistan combined occupy 54.7% of Kashmir whereas Indian-controlled Kashmir has an area of 38,830 sq. miles (45.3%).

The issue of Kashmir is very sensitive. Since the dispute started with Kashmir's accession to India on October 27, 1947, there have been many proposals for a solution, but no proposal has yet been acceptable to all three parties: India, Pakistan, and the people of Kashmir.

On the one hand, India considers Kashmir an integral part of itself, based on Hari Singh's legal accession. On the other hand, Pakistan asserts that the accession to India is not final until the Kashmiri people decide Kashmir's accession to either India or Pakistan through a plebiscite under the supervision of the United Nations.

This dispute over the territory of Kashmir has already triggered two wars—in 1947-48 and 1965—between the two countries and smaller clashes in 1999. Despite these two intense wars, neither country has succeeded in capturing the whole of Kashmir. A third war in 1971 ended in the creation of a Line of Control. Currently, the Line of Control separates the Indian and Pakistani armies. The people of Kashmir live with increasing threats of violence, terrorism, and instability. India and Pakistan, both armed with nuclear weapons, remain entangled in the Kashmir conflict. The threat of a nuclear war in the Indian subcontinent has increased with the nuclear testing in both India and Pakistan.

There is a great concern in the world that the dispute over Kashmir could trigger a nuclear war between India and Pakistan. The history of Pakistan reveals that whenever it came under a militarily controlled government, it favored a military solution for the Kashmir issue. The prospect of a peaceful solution increases with a democratically elected civil government in Pakistan.

It is significant to note that on July 2, 1972, India and Pakistan signed the Shimla Agreement under which both countries resolved to respect the Line of Control (LoC). The Line of Control has, in fact, been a *de facto* border for over 50 years. The masses in both Pakistani Kashmir and Indian Kashmir face distressing levels of poverty, pollution, illiteracy, unemployment, disease, and malnutrition. There could be no better approach to peace than to take such practical measures as would build the trust and confidence of Kashmiri people.

As a result of horrible violence in Kashmir, most Kashmiri *pandits* fled from their homeland. What was once a population of nearly 350,000 in the Valley of Kashmir has now been reduced to a mere 8,000. The Kashmir region will regain its normalcy only when its refugees feel safe to return home.

The dispute over Kashmir's accession to India has been standing in the way of the lasting peace and prosperity of the Indian subcontinent. The time is now ripe for the Indian subcontinent to become economically strong and politically united. The irrational hatred between Hindus and Muslims must be uprooted. There has to be overall development in the Indian subcontinent through the promotion of democracy.

A peaceful solution guided by a concern for the greater welfare of human beings needs to be sought. To this end, the best solution to the Kashmir issue is to start with the creation of a regional union of neighboring nations including India and Pakistan, with each member nation committed to democracy and respect for human rights. This regional union is described later in this chapter under the section "Proposing an 'Indus Union'." Once a regional "Indus Union" along the lines of the European Union is structured, mobility among various people will increase and the national borders will lose their significance. The proposed "Indus Union" will help create an atmosphere of harmony, unity, and prosperity. The Secretary-General of the United Nations "has consistently expressed his readiness to facilitate the search for an overall solution."[42]

5. Tibet's Spiritual Link with India

When the British left the Indian subcontinent in August 1947, Tibet was an independent country. On October 7, 1950, China, one of the world's greatest military powers, invaded the peaceful Buddhist nation of Tibet. The 14th **Dalai Lama, Tenzin Gyatso,** escaped in disguise from Lhasa, the capital of Tibet, on the evening of March 17, 1959. He crossed the border into India on March 30, 1959. About 85,000 Tibetans followed him across the Himalayas into exile. India granted the Dalai Lama and his followers asylum.

As the head of the Tibetan government-in-exile in Dharamsala, a town in Himachal Pradesh, India, the Dalai Lama declared Tibet's occupation by China illegal, brutal, and unjust. However, China holds that its relation with Tibet is a purely internal affair, because Tibet is, and has for centuries been, an integral part of China. Despite the fact that Tibet was an independent, sovereign country for much of its history and was ruled peacefully by its Buddhist Lamas, many countries currently recognize Tibet as a part of China. The **Dalai Lama**, who received the Nobel Prize for Peace in 1989 for his nonviolent opposition to Chinese rule in Tibet, has argued for the return of Tibet's freedom: "Also in the case of Tibet, because it was independent until 1950, the Chinese signed the 17-point Agreement with the Tibetan government. No other Chinese-occupied nationality has any such agreement, pact or treaty with China."[43]

Tibet has strong spiritual ties with India. The plight of the Tibetans is a human tragedy. India feels a sense of responsibility for the future of the Buddhist Lamas. It is well-known that Lord Buddha, the founder of Buddhism, was born in India. Buddhism reached Tibet from India through Ladakh.

Today, Ladakh, a part of Kashmir in India, is far more Tibetan than Tibet itself.

The unique Tibetan Buddhist heritage is threatened with extinction. To survive as a cultural and religious entity is a basic right of the peaceful Tibetan Buddhists. Under the auspices of the United Nations with a solid support of an "Indus Union," which is proposed later in the section "Proposing an 'Indus Union'," the Dalai Lama could negotiate more effectively with China.

6. Afghanistan's Sacred Tie with India

Just as Kashmir and Pakistan were an integral part of India before the Partition in 1947, so was Afghanistan during the rule of King Ashoka, also known as Ashoka the Great (321 BC– 270 BC), in the 4th century BC **Jawaharlal Nehru,** a world-renowned Indian statesman, wrote: "Indeed, for long stretches of time Afghanistan had been, and was destined to be, a part of India. Their language, Pashto, was basically derived from Sanskrit. . . . more correctly, the Afghans should be called the Indo-Afghans."[44] Writing about Afghanistan, **Jawaharlal Nehru** further noted: "In this conception, a large part of modern Afghanistan, then called Gandhara (from which comes the name of the present city of Kandahar), which was considered an integral part of the country, was included. Indeed the queen of the principal ruler was named Gandhari, the lady from Gandhara."[45]

Revealing an astounding fact that the Mahabharata War of 3139 BC was fought near Kabul in Afghanistan, **Satyananda**, one of India's greatest spiritual masters of the 20th century, concluded: "In the same way, the land on which the Mahabharata was fought is now in Afghanistan. Kurukshetra is not here in what is known as present-day India."[46] **Satyananda** continued: "Today, if archaeologists were to go to Afghanistan, find those coins, and ruins, and thus confirm the reality of Kurukshetra, even then the majority of people would not believe them. But there is an intellectual class of scientists and historians who would believe it."[47] If scholars and religious leaders accept Satyananda's conclusion, Afghanistan could very well be regarded as the sacred birthplace of the Bhagavad Gita.

7. Spiritual and Cultural Roots of India

Around 2500 BC, the Indus Valley civilization flourished in what today are Pakistan and India. It was a great civilization whose Sanskrit grammar, poetry, and ideas were highly evolved. The word "Hindu" refers to the religion and culture of the people who lived along the banks of the Indus River. The Persian invaders, who entered through the northwestern passes of the Himalayas, called the inhabitants on the eastern side of the *Sindhu* (Indus) River as *Sindhus* (Indians). Eventually, the "S" was pronounced as "H," and the word *Sindhu* became Hindu. Outside the Indian subcontinent, a person is generally considered a Hindu (Indian) if that person is from India, Pakistan, Bangladesh, Sri Lanka, Nepal, or Bhutan.

The history of caste prejudices has stained the honor of Hindus in the world. **Rama Tirtha** observed: "In the beginning, all the Hindus worked unitedly, without any caste prejudices whatsoever. Individuals took up work which they could perform with utmost efficiency. It was purely a system of division of labor, in the interest of efficiency. In course of time, however, this division of labor degenerated and distorted the very structure of our society which ultimately, adopted the baneful form of permanent casteism."[48]

In India's past, the cultural identities were not Hindu or Muslim, but were multicultural. **Yogananda** commented: "Countless Hindus and Muslims, now as in the past, have lived side by side in amity. Men of both faiths, in immense numbers, became disciples of the 'creedless' master Kabir (1450–1518); and to this day he has millions of followers (*Kabir-panthis*)."[49]

Despite hundreds of years of oppression, foreign

invasions, and tyranny, the subcontinent of India has been able to survive because of the influence of its spiritual masters. The Indian subcontinent has continually given rise to brilliant saints and sages who played a tremendous role in building up the civilization and culture so precious to people there. For generations, both Hindus and Muslims have been living peacefully side by side by obeying spiritual masters such as Nizamuddin, Amir Khusro, Ramananda, Kabir, Chaitanya Mahaprabhu, Mirabai, Rahim, Lalon Fakir, Bulleh Shah, Abu Yazid Al-Bistami, Mansoor Mastana, Saint Jnaneshwar, Guru Nanak, Saint Tukaram, Ramakrishna Paramahansa, Sai Baba of Shirdi, Nityananda of Ganeshpuri, Muktananda, Ramana Maharshi, Rama Tirtha, Neem Karoli Baba, and many others.

It is significant to note that Hindus and Muslims worked together to overthrow the British rule in India. Interestingly, even today more Muslims live in India than in Pakistan. As in America, in India religion is separate from state. The creation of Pakistan was based on the flawed notion that Hindus and Muslims cannot coexist in one nation. In fact, Pakistanis live peacefully with Indians in every part of the world.

Historically, the geographical boundaries of ancient India have become smaller and smaller. Foreign rulers succeeded in keeping people segregated so that they would remain dependent upon them. **Rama Tirtha** observed: "The Divide and Conquer policy of the rulers widens the gulf between Hindus and Mohammedans, and again between the different sects of Hindus. If India is to be saved, whether spiritually, politically, socially or in any way, it is to be saved through the kind of culture which removes discord and difference, which knocks at the head of caste-division, which deals a death-blow to jealousy and laziness. These are to be eradicated from India if we wish that she should stand up, live again, hold its own against other nations and be a source of blessing to England, to America, and to the whole world."[50]

8. Proposing an "Indus Union"

If Europe can have one Euro currency, why cannot Asia? Following the pattern of the European Union, it is time to unify the economies of India, Pakistan, Afghanistan, Nepal, Bhutan, Bangladesh, Sri Lanka, the Maldives, Myanmar (known as Burma until 1989), and others that were once an integral part of India into an "Indus Union." Southern Asia can become unified just as Europe has become unified as the European Union. Southern Asia can prosper immensely by working toward a common currency, visa, trade, and transportation system. This **will dramatically lessen its defense expenditure**, bringing peace and prosperity to the Indian subcontinent. The cultural bonds among South Asians, shaped through millennia of history, are much stronger than their superficial religious and ethnic differences.

If the "Indus Union" became a reality, production could be expected to easily support the current population. With a combined population of over 1.4 billion people (China: 1.3 billion; World: 6.3 billion), these neighboring nations together **would become the world's largest consumer market**, attracting unprecedented levels of commerce and investment from foreign countries. The introduction of a common currency, say "Indo," will enable people, services, investments, and products to move freely among the participating countries.

Participating countries should demonstrate a respect for human rights. **Jimmy Carter**, former U.S. President and recipient of the 2002 Nobel Prize for Peace, said: "My concept of human rights has grown to include not only the right to live in peace, but also to adequate health care, shelter, food, and to economic opportunity."[51]

Among the countries of the Indian subcontinent, there is more that unites than divides. The proposed unification is in the mutual interest of all the neighboring nations. In fact, it is an economic necessity. People of these nations need to realize the following advantages:

Table I: Poverty Level, Population, Land Area, and Defense
Expenditure 2002 in the Indian Subcontinent

Source: *The World Almanac and Book of Facts 2003 and 2004*

Nation	Annual GDP 2002 per capita (U.S. $)	Population 2002 (thousands)	Land Area (square miles)	Defense Exp. 2002 (billion $)
India	2,540	1,045,845	1,147,954	15.600
Pakistan	2,100	147,663	300,665	2.600
Afghanistan	700	27,756	250,001	.250
Bangladesh	1,700	133,377	51,703	.678
Sri Lanka	3,700	19,577	24,996	.645
Maldives	3,900	320	116	.036
Nepal	1,400	25,874	52,819	.070
Bhutan	1,300	2,094	18,147	.019
Myanmar (Burma)	1,660	42,238	253,955	.555
Total	N/A	1,444,744	2,100,356	20.453

Note: Gross Domestic Product (GDP) is the market value of all
goods and services produced in a country in one year.

GDP per capita, which is GDP divided by the number of people
in the country, provides a rough estimate of living standard in a
country. Less than $1 per day ($365 per person per year) is widely
used as a global standard of absolute poverty.

With the annual GDP per capita of $37,600 in 2002, the USA is
among the richest countries in the world, followed closely by
Norway, Switzerland, Japan, Denmark, and Sweden.

1. The Indus Union will bring lasting peace to the entire Indian subcontinent by providing the most effective solution to the Kashmir dispute between Pakistan and India.

2. The Indus Union will end the deadly arms race. Imagine how much better the condition of people would be if the money spent on combined defense budgets — nearly $20 billion in 2002 — were used to reduce the desperate poverty of the people in the subcontinent.

3. The Indus Union will effectively reunite divided families across the borders of India, Pakistan, and Bangladesh. Both Hindus and Muslims there share the same cultural heritage and aspirations. Historians note that the ancestors of most Pakistan and Bangladesh Muslims were originally Hindus who were converted to Islam.

4. The Indus Union will be large enough to create such stability as would allow people to live securely, move freely, and support their families. Neighboring nations are too small to do that on their own.

5. The Indus Union will be unified enough to develop and progress independent of external influences.

6. The Indus Union will be big enough to become the world's largest consumer market. Creating a single currency, perhaps 'Indo,' in the Indian subcontinent will go a long way in coordinating these neighboring nations.

7. The Indus Union will encourage technical, commercial, and industrial collaboration among the member countries.

8. The Indus Union will be large enough for the optimal utilization and distribution of natural resources like water, electricity, and minerals.

9. The Indus Union will be strong enough to deal with global human diseases, such as AIDS.

10. The Indus Union will promote cultural exchange in fields such as music, literature, arts, sports, and cinema.

11. The Indus Union will improve education and training.

12. The Indus Union will provide greater job and investment opportunities.

13. The Indus Union will help modernize highways, railways, and airports.

14. The Indus Union will promote travel, tourism, and pilgrimages.

In conclusion, the Indus Union will become much more than the sum of its parts.

9. A 5,000-Year Cycle Predicts Asia's Prosperity

Rama Tirtha, who was not only a spiritual master but also a brilliant mathematician, predicted prosperity for the Indian subcontinent by explaining cycles of time called the Law of Periodicity. **Rama Tirtha** observed: "Everything in this world moves rhythmically, and the Law of Periodicity governs all phenomena."[52] Nature shows that the sun moves from east to west, coming back to the east to begin a new cycle.

In accordance with this law, financial prosperity has been moving in the past 5,000 years from the peak of civilization in India. Prosperity passed through Persia, Assyria, and further west to Egypt; next came the turn for Greece; after that, Rome, and then Germany, France, and Spain; then it traveled to Great Britain. It did not stop there; it traveled further west to America. In America itself, prosperity traveled westward starting from the east coast, until it reached California. Now prosperity has crossed over the Pacific Ocean with the cycle of prosperity turning back to the east. In the Far East, Japan has already become a prosperous country.

Rama Tirtha predicted: "After Japan, China will rise and gain prosperity and strength. After China, the sun of prosperity and learning will again smile at India."[53] When this Law of

Periodicity comes full circle, then the Indian subcontinent may dazzle the whole world with its forthcoming prosperity. In all likelihood, the Indian subcontinent would now help the rest of the world with its learning and technology.

10. Secret to Peace and Prosperity

The new generation is more interested in financial prosperity, yoga, and the Internet than in the politics of war. Having slept long enough under the influence of ignorance, inaction, and disunity, it is time for the Indian subcontinent to regain power, prestige, and dignity. The key to improving the standard of living is to achieve a literacy rate of one hundred percent. People have to fall in love with science and technology. By creating a more literate society, both unemployment and overpopulation can be significantly reduced. This goal can be achieved only by uniting people.

All differences based on religion and the caste system, need to be completely uprooted by mutual love, respect, and harmony — however difficult the task may be. The secret to attaining peace and prosperity is harmonious unity. In the words of **Sivananda**: "Realize first your unity with all the members of your family, then with all the members of your community, then with all the members of your district, then with all the members of your state, then with all the members of the whole nation, then with all the people of the whole world. If you succeed in this attempt, then only can you realize your unity or oneness with God."[54]

The democratic reunification of nations in the Indian subcontinent is a great step toward permanent peace in the region. The idea of reunifying nations may at first sound unachievable, but it is like a seed that grows into a mighty tree. It is a solid stride toward becoming a great economic power in the world. **Sri Aurobindo** (1872–1950), one of the glorious spiritual masters of India, in his message broadcast over All India Radio, Tiruchchirappalli, on August 15, 1947, said: "For unification is a necessity of Nature, an inevitable movement.

Its necessity for the nations is also clear, for without it the freedom of the small nations may be at any moment in peril, and the life even of the large and powerful nations insecure. The unification is therefore to the interests of all, and only human imbecility and stupid selfishness can prevent it."[55]

Chapter 3

Yoga: The Highest of All Unions

Swami Vivekananda (1863–1902)

CHAPTER 3
Yoga:
The Highest of All Unions

In the present age, with its emphasis on the material sciences, spiritual ideas are generally looked upon as fictitious or mythical. However, spiritual concepts are not necessarily unscientific or irrational. In fact, spiritual concepts are part of an entire science of yoga that has been laid out as systematically as any modern science. Declaring yoga as a science, **Yogananda** wrote: "All creation is governed by law. The principles that operate in the outer universe, discoverable by scientists, are called natural laws. But there are subtler laws that rule the hidden spiritual planes and the inner realm of consciousness; these principles are knowable through the science of yoga."[56]

It is not rational to deny the assertions about yoga unless yoga has actually been practiced. **Sri Chinmoy** (1931-present), a renowned spiritual master, said: "There are many things that are not visible in the outer plane and yet are absolutely real. If you have seen your soul or your psychic being, how can science deny it? We adore science because science has discovered many, many things. But we cannot deny the things that spiritual persons have discovered and have made others see."[57] Many world-acclaimed spiritual giants such as Vivekananda (1863–1902), Rama Tirtha (1873–1906), Yogananda (1893–1952), and Muktananda (1908–1982) traveled to the USA and other parts of the world to help people through yoga.

1. What Is Yoga?

Yoga, the science of the soul, is an offshoot of ancient tantra. The word "tantra" stems from two words: "tanoti" meaning expansion of the mind, and "trayati" meaning

Ardha-narisvara, the male-female principle

liberation of energy from the mind. *Vijnana Bhairava Tantra*, written about four thousand years ago, is considered to be the authoritative text book on tantra. It contains 112 techniques for experiencing the divine Self.

Yoga is often translated as mysticism. The Sanskrit word "yoga"is derived from the root, *yujir*, to unite, meaning the mystic union between the individual soul and the universal Spirit. In essence, the individual soul is identical with the universal Spirit. This union already exists, but one may not be aware of it. Therefore, Self-awareness is practiced in yoga. This practice of Self-awareness can transform a human mind into divine consciousness.

The concept behind yoga is the same as the process of fusion, described in modern physics. **Fusion** happens when two opposite forces leave their positions of polarity to move toward the center, and at one point, they unite. Opposite forces, such as positive and negative, *prakasha* and *vimarsha*, yang and yin, *pingala* and *ida*, *shukra* and *raja*, changeless and changeful, passive and active, plus and minus, space and time, knower and known, unmanifest and manifest, *Ham* and *Sa*, denote the two sides or duality of the same reality. In yoga, the names used for these two opposite forces are: *shiva* (*purusha*) and *shakti* (*prakriti*). *Shiva* is universal consciousness, the seer of all that exists. *Shakti* is energy or Nature, which means everything that is seen. The separation between the seer and the seen is called **fission**, the direct opposite of fusion.

In fusion, duality dissolves. The natural process by which duality dissolves can be described as follows:

At the gross level, the earth element becomes absorbed into the water element, the water into the fire, the fire into the air, the air into the ether, and the ether into the conscious mind. So continuing, at the subtle level, the conscious mind merges into the intellect, the intellect into the unconscious mind, the unconscious mind into the ego, and finally, the ego merges into the divine Self, the seer. When the seen completely merges into the seer, there is supreme bliss of one's own true nature.

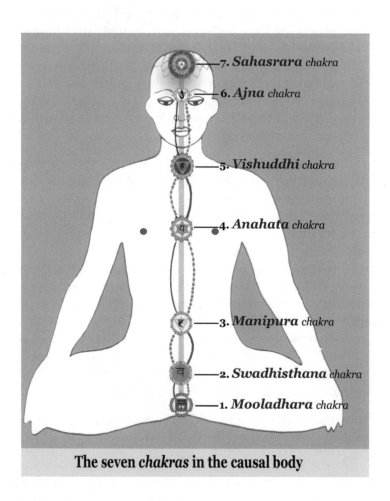

7. *Sahasrara* chakra

6. *Ajna* chakra

5. *Vishuddhi* chakra

4. *Anahata* chakra

3. *Manipura* chakra

2. *Swadhisthana* chakra

1. *Mooladhara* chakra

The seven *chakras* in the causal body

This spiritual bliss is true yoga. In every realm of Nature, it is the union between two opposites that creates bliss or life.

According to modern psychology, everyone is both masculine and feminine. In other words, there is woman in man and man in woman. Unique to Hindu mythology is a single form of half-male and half-female called *Ardha-narisvara*. Like two sides of the same coin, *shiva* and *shakti* are opposite sides of one Supreme Reality. ***Shakti* — the universal energy — residing in the human body is called *kundalini*.** She is the active aspect of the Absolute. When *kundalini* awakes, it rises from the base of the spine in the *mooladhara* and unites with *shiva* at the top of the head in the *sahasrara*. A nectar-like coolness, as it were, coming from hundreds of moons starts flowing from this union of *shiva* and *shakti*. Thus, the individual Self merges into the universal Spirit — the subtlest union of the masculine and the feminine within. **This ultimate union of *shiva* and *shakti* occurring at the top of the head is called yoga,** love, *samadhi*, Self-realization, enlightenment, liberation, *moksha*, *nirvana*, *kaivalya*, emancipation, whole, or truth. Indeed, it is the highest of all unions.

2. *Kundalini* Awakening

Kundalini, the power of the inner Self, is a potential spiritual energy inherent in every human being. Yoga can be effortlessly achieved by awakening and channeling *kundalini*, which is loacted in the subtle body, not in the physical body. The subtle body is within this physical body like the bladder inside a soccer ball. It is an exact counterpart of the physical body. Without the subtle body, the physical body cannot survive. The seat of *kundalini* is exactly midpoint from the sole of the foot to the top of the head.

It is said that no super conscious state or *samadhi* is ever possible without the *kundalini* awakening. Although the word *kundalini* originated in India, the *kundalini* awakening experience is common to all religions. For example, in Christianity, it is called the "Holy Spirit."

Kundalini awakening is a divine gift of God received through the medium of a Guru (true spiritual master). By the look, touch, word, or thought, a Guru can fully unfold the *kundalini* in a worthy seeker. In yoga, this *kundalini* awakening is called *shaktipat*. For instance, the initiation that Vivekananda received from Ramakrishna Paramahansa was *shaktipat*. *Kundalini* yoga is also known by various names such as, *maha* yoga, *siddha* yoga, *shaktipat* yoga, *gurukripa, gurumarga, sahaja* yoga, *kriya* yoga, *purna* yoga, or the perfect yoga.

Kundalini, functioning on the physical plane, is called *hatha* yoga, on the plane of speech, mantra yoga, and on the mental plane, *laya* yoga. Explaining the effect of *shaktipat* initiation, **Muktananda** said: "As we follow *Siddha* yoga, these various yogas (*Raja* yoga, *Mantra* yoga, *Laya* yoga, *Hatha* yoga, and *Dhyana* yoga) happen to a person without his practicing them. Without his trying to learn them, they just come to him. This is the result of *kundalini* awakening. Just as nobody deliberately pushes the outgoing breath out or pulls the incoming breath in — it happens by itself — in the same way this yoga is self-generated and self-sustained. You don't have to do anything; you just sit back and watch it happen to you. This comes from *shaktipat* initiation."[58]

In the *sahasrara* (the cerebral center at the top of the head), there is a sparkling tiny **blue light**, which an individual can see only after the awakening of *kundalini*. It is the vibration of this blue light that controls breathing in every human being. What is called death is nothing but the departure of this blue light from the physical body.

In *Kundalini* yoga, all aspects of yoga come automatically to a seeker whose *kundalini* is awakened. Then the seeker's entire personality — actions, emotions, mind, and intellect — starts to develop. The inner realms open up. Knowledge arises from within. The seeker radiates love and feels extraordinary bliss. This *kundalini* energy is a fact, not myth or fiction. Indeed, *Kundalini* yoga is a complete yoga.

Physical, mental, or emotional movements initiated by

the awakened *kundalini* are called *kriyas* in yoga. Explaining *kriyas*, **Muktananda** wrote: "Some of the *kriyas* are a part of *Raja* yoga, some of *Hatha* yoga, some of *Mantra* yoga, and some of *Bhakti* yoga, for when the power of the Guru enters the disciple, all these yogas occur spontaneously according to the disciple's needs. When all four yogas come together to work within the disciple, this is called *Siddha* yoga or *Maha* yoga."[59]

With the awakening of *kundalini*, dormant compartments in the brain start blossoming like flowers. The faculty of intuition, which remains dormant in most people, starts developing. This awakening generates electrical impulses, which are intimately connected with the entire brain. Yogis hold that **psychic energy and physical energy are convertible into each other.** To energize the whole brain, the following psychic energy centers called *chakras* need to be activated:

1. *Mooladhara* — **Earth** or survival center; corresponds to coccygeal plexus; connected to the sense of smell; 4 petaled deep **red** lotus at the base of the spinal column.

2. *Swadhisthana* — **Water** or social center; corresponds to the prostatic plexus; connected to the sense of taste; 6 petaled **orange** lotus at the root of the genital organ.

3. *Manipura* — **Fire** or will center; corresponds to the solar plexus; connected to the sight; 10 petaled bright **yellow** lotus in the naval region.

4. *Anahata* — **Air** or heart center; corresponds to the cardiac plexus; connected to the sense of touch; 12 petaled **blue** lotus in the heart region.

5. *Vishuddhi* — **Ether** or throat center; corresponds to the cervical plexus; connected to the sense of audition; 16 petaled **purple** lotus at the base of the throat.

6. *Ajna* — **Mind** or third-eye center; corresponds to the cavernous plexus; 2 petaled **silver-grey** lotus in the middle of the two eyebrows.

7. *Sahasrara* — **Consciousness** or crown center; corresponds to the cerebrum; 1,000 petaled **multicolored** lotus.

Though the *chakras* are located in the subtle body, their influence extends to the physical body. **Sivananda** remarked: "Just because post-mortem examination of the body does not reveal these *chakras* in the spinal column, some people think that these *chakras* do not exist at all, and are merely the fabrication of a fertile brain. This attitude reminds us of a doctor who declared that he had performed many post-mortems and had never yet discovered a soul!"[60]

When *kundalini* is awakened, either by yogic practices or by the Guru's grace, it activates all these *chakras* as it travels up from the *Mooladhara* to the *Sahasrara*. The most important nerve (*nadi*) in the subtle body of a human being is *sushumna*, which extends from the base of the spine to the top of the head. Within the *sushumna* nerve, there is a fine nerve called *vajra*. Within this *vajra* nerve, there is a very fine nerve known as *chitra*. In the *chitra* is the finest nerve called *brahma*. It is this *brahma* nerve that is the passage for *kundalini* and contains all the *chakras*. For a comprehensive knowledge of these *chakras*, readers are referred to *Science of the Soul* by Yogeshwaranand Saraswati and Swami Vyasdev (published by Yoga Niketan Trust, New Delhi, India) as well as Sir John Woodroffe's *The Serpent Power* (published by Dover Publications, Inc., New York).

3. Is Yoga a Religion?

There seems to be a lot of confusion about the relationship between yoga and religion. Peace of mind is the central note in yoga. There is a reservoir of peace within each of us. The practice of yoga is meant to tap this reservoir. Yoga brings tranquility and energy to a person, whether he or she belongs to a particular religion or no religion at all. Those who believe that yoga is Hinduism are terribly mistaken. Although yoga was discovered in ancient India, it belongs to humanity.

Yoga is a way of life aimed at manifesting the dormant divine power in a human being. **Yogananda** observed: "Many uninformed persons speak of yoga as *Hatha* yoga or consider yoga to be 'magic,' dark mysterious rites for attaining spectacular powers. When scholars, however, speak of yoga they mean the system expounded in *Yoga Sutras* (also known as Patanjali's Aphorisms): *Raja* ('royal') yoga."[61]

Yoga is not just stretching the body. It is concerned with consciousness. In yoga, one delves deeply into one's own inner consciousness. It leads to a state similar to conscious sleep. There is no difference in Christian, Hindu, or Muslim sleep. If the sleep state is not considered a religion, how could yoga be a religion?

The effects of yoga are being proven through scientific experimentation. Yoga is a practical science that can be taught in schools and colleges. Just as any Jew, Christian, Muslim, or Hindu accepts biology and physics, an individual should be able to accept yoga as a science. Speaking about yoga as the science of the soul, **Rama Tirtha** wrote: "All the religions of this world are based upon a personality. Christianity hinges around the name of Christ, Confucianism around the name of Confucius, Buddhism around the name of Buddha, Zoroastrianism around the name of Zoroaster, Mohammedanism around the name of Mohammad. The word Vedanta means the ultimate science, the science of the soul, and it requires a man to approach it in the same spirit in which you approach a work on chemistry. You don't read a work on chemistry, taking it on the authority of chemists like Lavoisier, Boyle, Reynolds, Davy and others. You take up a work on chemistry and analyze everything yourself. Rama believes that water consists of hydrogen and oxygen on the authority of his own experiments, not on the authority of anybody else."[62]

Yoga is a source of energy in life. More and more people all over the world are practicing yoga for its benefits:

1. On a physical level, yoga postures strengthen the

body, improving health.

2. On a psychological level, yoga sharpens the intellect, aiding concentration.

3. On a spiritual level, yoga awakens one's divinity, developing intuition.

4. Patanjali, the Scientist of the Absolute

The yoga of Patanjali, the foremost authority on yoga, is concerned with the mind. It is known as *Raja* yoga, *Ashtanga* (eight-limbed) yoga, or simply yoga.

Although Patanjali's actual birth date is unknown, **Satyananda** disclosed: "He was a contemporary of Buddha, that is, he lived 2,500 years ago."[63] Reflecting on Patanjali's greatness, **Yogananda** wrote: "If you tell people that you are following a Hindu religion — or for that matter, any religion other than their own — prejudice immediately arises in their minds. But Patanjali goes beyond all personalities and dogmas. He states that yoga is the heart of all religions; it is the science of religion, by which the true principles of religion can be proven with exact and known results. Yoga fulfills the purpose of religion: achievement of oneness or union with God — the ultimate necessity of every soul."[64]

Patanjali wrote *Yoga Sutras*, which has four chapters: Chapter I *Samadhi* (Awareness) — 51 verses, Chapter II *Sadhana* (Practice) — 55 verses, Chapter III *Vibhuti* (Supernatural Powers) — 56 verses, and Chapter IV *Kaivalya* (Liberation) — 34 verses.

The *Yoga Sutras* not only reveals mysteries of the human mind but also explains techniques for concentrating the mind. The greater the power of concentration, the subtler the manifestation of knowledge. Knowledge is relative when it is acquired through the mind and its senses. But, when this knowledge takes place without the aid of the mind and its senses, it becomes intuitive and absolute. Only Spirit, which is changeless, can be taken as the absolute constant by which all perceptions can be measured.

According to Einstein's General Theory of Relativity, experience of space and time is relative to light velocity, which Einstein took as a constant. **Declaring that the Einstein's constant is not really absolute**, **Yogananda** wrote: "Light velocity is a mathematical standard or constant not because there is an absolute value in 186,300 miles a second, but because no material body, whose mass increases with its velocity, can ever attain the velocity of light. Stated another way: only a material body whose mass is infinite could equal the velocity of light. This conception brings us to the law of miracles. Masters who are able to materialize and dematerialize their bodies and other objects, and to move with the velocity of light, and to utilize the creative light rays in bringing into instant visibility any physical manifestation, have fulfilled the lawful condition: their mass is infinite."[65]

Patanjali's *Yoga Sutras* reveals the super conscious state called *samadhi* (transcendental awareness) in which a yogi's awareness is absolute, not relative. Modern psychology recognizes only three states: conscious, subconscious, and unconscious. The fourth state is "super conscious," which is recognized only in yoga. Therefore, Patanjali can be recognized as a scientist of the Absolute for his *Yoga Sutras*, which goes far beyond Einstein's general theory of relativity. In the words of **Vivekananda**: "The Yogis say that man can go beyond his direct sense-perception and beyond his reason also. Man has in him the faculty, the power, of transcending his intellect even, a power which is in every being, every creature. By the practice of Yoga that power is aroused, and then man transcends the ordinary limits of reason, and directly perceives things which are beyond all reason."[66]

5. Patanjali's Yoga Sutras

Patanjali's aphorisms explain a classical system by which one gains complete mastery of the mind. The *Yoga Sutras*, chapter 1, verse 2, reads:

योगश्चित्तवृत्तिनिरोधः ।

"Yogash chittavritti-nirodhah"

This means the purpose of yoga is to stop the *vrittis* (modifications) of the mind. Such a state of the mind can be attained by the continuous repetition of a sound or vibration called mantra. The modifications of the mind are classified under five headings:

1.   *Pramana* — valid knowledge:

     (i) direct perception;

     (ii) inferences; and

     (iii) authoritative testimony (words of others in whom we have faith).

2.   *Viparyaya* — illusive knowledge like that of a mirage.

3.   *Vikalpa* — fantasy.

4.   *Nidra* — sleep without dreams.

5.   *Smriti* — memory.

The mind is an element that is even finer than ether. In yoga, the mind (*chitta*) is called *antahkarana* (inner organ), which is made up of three components: *manas* (thought), *buddhi* (intellect), and *ahamkara* (ego). *Manas* is the reporting faculty that receives reports in the forms of thoughts, desires, passions, emotions, sentiments, and memory. *Buddhi* is the deciding faculty that reacts to these reports in the forms of reasoning, discrimination, and inferences. *Ahamkara* is the ego sense that claims these reports as its own. It is as if an electric light bulb is declaring: "I am the electric current."

The mind (*chitta*) and its modifications (*vrittis*) are not synonymous. The mind always expresses itself in the form of modifications. The aim of *Raja yoga* is to calm these modifications through concentration, meditation, and absorption. Comparing modifications (*vrittis*), mind (*chitta*), and the inner Self (*atman*), **Vivekananda** wrote in his book *Raja Yoga*: "The bottom of a lake we cannot see, because its surface is covered with ripples. It is only possible for us to catch a glimpse of the bottom when the ripples have subsided, and the water is calm. If the water is muddy, or is agitated all the time, the bottom will not be seen. If it is clear, and there are no waves, we shall see the bottom. The bottom of the lake is our own true Self; the lake is the *chitta*, the waves are the *vrittis*."[67]

6. The Eight Steps in Yoga

The whole syllabus of *Raja* yoga is meant to train the human mind gradually and thoroughly. Briefly, the following are the eight systematic steps or progressive stages that apply not only to *Raja* yoga but also to all types of yoga:

1. **Yama** or Social Discipline:

   (i) **Ahimsa** (thou shall not injure);

   (ii) **Satya** (thou shall not lie);

   (iii) **Asteya** (thou shall not steal);

   (iv) **Brahmacharya**[h] (thou shall not be lustful); and

   (v) **Aparigraha** (thou shall not be greedy).

2. **Niyama** or Personal Discipline:

   (i) **Saucha** (thou shalt be clean);

   (ii) **Santosha** (thou shalt be content);

   (iii) **Tapas** (thou shalt be self-controlled);

   (iv) **Svadhyaya** (thou shalt be studious); and

---

[h] According to Sivananda, *Brahmacharya* means the control of the pituitary center in the brain from which the sexual hormones (*retas*) flow.

(v) **Ishvara pranidhana** (thou shalt devote to God).

3. **Asana**: firm, comfortable meditation posture.

4. **Pranayama**: control of *Prana* or life force. The **ten** states of *Prana* that sustains a human body are:

(i) **prana** (exhaling, works the sensory nerves);

(ii) **apana** (inhaling, works the excretory system);

(iii) **samana** (works the digestive system);

(iv) **udana** (works the muscular system — it takes one to sleep; it separates the astral body from the physical body at death and leads to reincarnation; and it brings the experience of *samadhi*);

(v) **vyana** (works the circulatory system — circulates blood all over the body);

(vi) **naga** (belching and hiccup);

(vii) **kurma** (blinking of the eyes);

(viii) **krikara** (sneezing and coughing);

(ix) **devadatta** (yawning); and

(x) **dhananjaya** (causes decomposition of the physical body after death).

5. **Pratyahara**: withdrawal of the mind from the five senses — sound, touch, sight, taste, and smell.

6. **Dharana**: concentration of mind at any special point or object.

7. **Dhyana:** meditation on the inner Self.

8. **Samadhi**: absorption or union with Spirit.

The first four steps are collectively known as external practices, and the latter four are collectively known as internal practices. The first two steps, *Yama* and *Niyama*, are the Ten Commandments of yoga. The steps of *Asana* and *Pranayama* are collectively known as *Hatha* yoga.

7. Supernatural Powers

Patanjali's *Sutras* describes various supernatural powers in its third chapter "*Vibhuti.*" The supernatural powers can be gained through the practice of *samyama*, which is defined as a deep mental state of *dharana* (concentration), *dhyan* (meditation), and *samadhi* (absorption) combined. According to Patanjali, the practice of *samyama* upon any object brings perfection concerning that object. For example, by the practice of *samyama* on the cavity of the throat, one can overcome hunger and thirst for a long period of time. A yogic power is both genuine and scientific.

Jesus possessed the yogic powers described in Patanjali's *Yoga Sutras*. Relating an instance of Jesus Christ's miraculous powers, **Rama Tirtha** wrote: "You know Christ did not die when he was crucified. This is a fact which may be proved. He was in a state called *Samadhi*, a state where all life-functions stop, where the pulse beats not, where the blood apparently leaves the veins, where all signs of life are no more, when the body is, as it were, crucified. Christ threw himself into that state for three days and like a yogi came to life again and made his escape and came back to live in Kashmir."[68]

Describing the yogic power of resurrection after six weeks of apparent death, **Yogananda** related this historical event: "Another miracle of Raja yoga was demonstrated when *Sadhu* [monk] Haridas permitted himself to be buried alive underground for six weeks. **In the nineteenth century, in the court of prince Ranjit Singh — emperor of the Punjab —** and under the seal of French and other European doctors, the miraculous performance of *Sadhu* Haridas was historically recorded. After Haridas's body was waxed all over, sewn securely in a sack, and then sealed in a stone chest, the emperor buried the *sadhu* several feet below the earth in the royal courtyard. Careful watch was maintained over the site for six weeks. Millions of people waited for the news about the *sadhu's* disinterment after the six weeks had passed. The stone chest was opened, the cloth and wax was removed, and the body was examined by French and English doctors and pronounced dead. Yet in a few minutes *Sadhu* Haridas blinked his eyes and came back to life. Boom! Went the cannon from the ramparts of the emperor's fort at Lahore [Punjab, India], heralding and declaring that saint Haridas was alive. In any comprehensive historical book on India this occurrence will be found recorded."[69]

The above examples in history, which you may or may not believe, clearly indicates the continuity of consciousness in spite of the suspension of breath. All these supernatural powers are like milestones that come automatically at a particular level as the mind evolves in the journey of yoga. In the words of **Yogananda**: "Emergence of the characteristic powers is evidence of the scientific structure of the yoga system, wherein delusive imaginations about one's 'spiritual progress' are banished; proof is required!"[70]

Remember that these miraculous powers are manifestations of the mind, not of the soul. Therefore, they may disappear one day. According to Patanjali, supernatural powers (*vibhutis*) impede Self-realization. **Yogananda** stated: "Patanjali warns the devotee that unity with Spirit should be the sole goal, not the possession of *vibhutis*—the merely incidental flowers along the sacred path. May the Eternal Giver be sought, not His phenomenal gifts! God does not reveal Himself to a seeker who is satisfied with any lesser attainment. The striving yogi is therefore careful not to exercise his phenomenal powers, lest they arouse false pride and distract him from entering the ultimate state of *Kaivalya* [Liberation]."[71]

8. What Is Meditation?

The seventh step on the ladder of *Raja* yoga is the meditation on the inner Self. The definition of meditation given by sage **Kapil** in his *Sankhya Darshan* is:

ध्यानं निर्विषयं मनः

Dhyanam nirwishyam manah
(Meditation is a thoughtless state of the mind.)

Meditation is for stilling the mind. The goal of meditation is to make the mind completely free from worldly thoughts. Only when the mind becomes totally silent is the state of meditation experienced. It is not easy to achieve such a state. It may sound paradoxical but it is true that such a thoughtless state can be achieved if the mind is filled with mantra (inner sound) for a long time.

Scientists, using an EEG (electroencephalograph) to depict brain waves, find that meditation helps one to control alpha, beta, and delta brainwaves. According to DK's *e.encyclopedia*: "When a person is awake but resting, the brain produces a regular pattern of medium-length waves — alpha waves. When alert and concentrating, the brain produces shorter, quicker waves — beta waves. During deep sleep, very long, slow delta waves occur."[72]

Speaking of tests conducted by the American scientists, **Satyananda** noted: "When subjects practicing a mantra like Om were exposed to ECG, EEG, and other machines, which register what is happening in the body, they found at the end of the practice that the brain waves had shifted from beta to alpha and that the heart, the lungs, the nervous system, and the brain as a whole, showed a very normal, healthy picture."[73]

Satyananda further stated: "When you sit in the lotus posture with your spine upright and straight and with your eyes closed, what happens? They have found brain waves altering, oxygen consumption changing, the respiratory system behaving differently, the metabolic rate, and the metabolic process undergoing great change, and the muscles of the heart improving. They have also found changes in the rate of regeneration in cells of the body."[74]

Meditation can help an individual overcome anger, irritation, lethargy, and lack of motivation. It can also free a person from evil influences. Indeed, meditation can transform a person's character, conduct, and behavior. Through the practice of meditation, lost energy is replenished, memory is improved, intellect is sharpened, and intuition is developed. Meditation removes all worries and tensions of the mind. The need for sleep decreases and there is awareness even during the dream state.

The best form of yoga is meditation. Everybody can practice it. Meditation on the inner Self makes our lives better, sharpens our worldly skills, and unfolds our love for others. An article in *TIME* entitled "Just Say OM" reads: "Scientists study it. Doctors recommend it. Millions of Americans—many of whom don't even own crystals—practice it every day. Why? Because meditation works."[75]

9. The Technique of Meditation

Vijnana Bhairava Tantra, an ancient treatise considered the supreme authority on meditation techniques, reveals 112 techniques for experiencing the meditation state. Here is the very first technique described in verse 24 of *Vijnana Bhairava Tantra*. It concerns breathing and is known as the *Hamsa* technique of meditation:

ऊर्ध्वे प्राणो ह्यधो जीवो विसर्गात्मा परोच्चरेत् ।

उत्पत्तिद्वितयस्थाने भरणाद भरिता स्थितिः ॥ २४ ॥

Urdhve prano hy adho jivo visargatma parocharet /
Utpattidvitayasthane bharanad bharita sthihi // 24 //

"Radiant one, this experience may dawn between two breaths. After breath comes in (down) and just before turning up (out)—the beneficence."[76]

Meditation is easy to practice if it is understood properly. Refer to **Table II**, which depicts meditation as a state in which an individual is both conscious and thoughtless. Between two breaths, there exist two gaps or spaces. The gap between the inbreath and the outbreath is the inner space (*antar kumbhaka*), whereas the gap between the outbreath and the inbreath is the outer space (*bahiranga kumbhaka*). Under the *Hamsa* technique, the highest meditation (*turiya*) can be experienced by focusing on either of these two spaces.

Man's need for sleep proves that turning within brings peace and contentment. When you turn your mind inward, you can experience your inner Self, your very own being. **Muktananda** said: "Through meditation you can know your own inner Self. That one who understands the most secret things inside you is the Self. For example, when you are in sleep there is someone who watches everything, who witnesses everything, who understands everything even though you are asleep. And then when you wake up, that being tells you what you have seen in your dream. That being is the Self, so meditate on the Self."[77]

To experience your own Self is the goal of meditation. We are all accustomed to turning inward in sleep. Just as you slip easily into sleep, so also you can glide into meditation. Successful meditation is the state of being both conscious and thoughtless—a state of wakeful sleep.

Sit in a comfortable posture, keeping your spine straight. Remain absolutely motionless. Close your eyes and become aware that your physical body is totally still and relaxed. Now focus on your own inner awareness. Identify yourself with your "I am" awareness, not with your physical body and your mind. Be peaceful, silent, and tranquil.

The breath can be used as a technique for reaching the meditation state. With awareness, simply follow your natural breath as it passes in and out of the nostrils. With inhalation, the abdomen expands, and with exhalation, it contracts. In his book, *I Am That*, **Muktananda** has revealed that we breathe 21,600 times in 24 hours, which averages 15 breaths per minute. The number 21,600 (108x200) with its multiples and integers is of great importance in time cycles. In a day,

Table II: Meditation: The State of Wakeful Sleep

Levels	State of Consciousness	Sanskrit Name	Condition	Awareness
1st state	Wakefulness	*Jagrat*	Not thoughtless but *conscious*	Conscious mind
2nd state	Dream sleep	*Swapna*	Not thoughtless but *conscious*	Conscious mind
3rd state	Dreamless sleep	*Susupti*	*Thoughtless* but not conscious	Unconscious mind
Ever-present background for *all* three states	Wakeful sleep called *Meditation*	*Turiya*	Both *thoughtless* and *conscious*	Beyond mind

there are 86,400 seconds, which is a multiple of 21,600. Further, one *Kali Yuga,* which began on February 18, 3102 BC, equals 432,000 years, a multiple of 21,600.

Our breathing is not merely inhaling oxygen and exhaling carbon dioxide. While breathing, our nervous system and brain are greatly affected. By gaining knowledge of the rhythms of the breath, explained in an ancient text called *Shiva Swarodaya,* one can effectively control the tendencies of the mind. It is found that when the left nostril is flowing freely, the right hemisphere of the brain concerned with intuition and creativity becomes active, and when the right nostril is flowing freely, the left hemisphere of the brain, which processes information logically, becomes active. When both nostrils are flowing freely, both hemispheres of the brain become active. The left nostril is considered the moon, called *ida,* and the right nostril the sun, called *pingala* in yoga. The breath alternates from *ida* to *pingala* every hour. When both nostrils flow freely, it is called the flow of *sushumna* and this is the best time for meditation practice.

Simply watching the breath can calm the mind. Therefore, practice unbroken awareness of the breath — the same breath that comes in, goes out. Move your awareness in with your breath and then move your awareness out with your breath, thus remaining fully conscious at all times. Between the in-breath and the out-breath, there is a center, junction, interval, or gap (called *sandhi* in Sanskrit), in which breathing ceases. What is most important is to maintain attentive awareness on the center of two breaths. Watch attentively to catch a glimpse of this gap. Let your awareness be unbroken. As your awareness becomes keen, suddenly you will recognize this gap. In the gap between two breaths, you are a pure being. If you can settle with full awareness into this gap, you are in meditation on your inner Self, the state of perfect stillness of the mind.

Let any thoughts arise in your mind. There are five stages of the mind from the lowest to the highest: disturbed (*ksipta*), dull (*mudha*), restless (*viksipta*), one-pointed (*ekagra*), and well-controlled (*niruddha*). Your present state of mind can be at any one of these stages. According to Patanjali, every mind, regardless of its present state, can become one-pointed (*ekagra*).

Negative thoughts such as bad feelings, anger, lust, worries, jealousy, and greed may arise during meditation. Like negative thoughts, there may be positive thoughts. Thoughts are objects whereas the "I am" awareness is the subject. Ask yourself: Who becomes aware of the thoughts that come and go? Just bring your focus on this subject, not on the objects. In other words, if thoughts arise, resume the "I am" awareness, which is the source of all your thoughts. During meditation, go after the subjective inner awareness, not the objective thoughts.

Just as clouds come and go in the sky without affecting the sky, so also various thoughts appear and disappear without affecting the purity of your inner Self. Your inner Self is completely separate from both your physical body and your mind. Once you know you are not the mind, you can then look at your mind's happenings. The practice of watching the mind's happenings is introspection. The most interesting thing about the mind is that if you introspect, the mind's happenings or thoughts start disappearing.

As you become watchful, memories and imaginations pass by. The past is memory and the future is imagination. Be in the present moment. Breathing is always in the present. Become aware of your breathing to be in the present.

When breathing in and out, a sound or vibration called mantra is created. What is the sound of your breath? You have to experience the sound for yourself. So attune your mind with your breath and listen to the sound. The ingoing breath (*apana*) sounds as "*ham,*" and the outgoing breath (*prana*) sounds as "*sa.*" It is the sound of the breath that is repeating this *Hamsa* mantra. It is a natural mantra, always going on within you, whether you are aware of it or not. *Hamsa* mantra means, "I am That." When you simply watch your natural breath, being aware that it is coming in with the sound *ham* and going out with the sound *sa,* you are truly practicing the *hamsa* technique of meditation. It is said that God originally manifested as Word or Sound. Since the source of sound is God, it can surely put you in touch with its source.

The repetition of the conscious mantra is the easiest way to meditate on the inner Self. The mantra that you receive from a fully Self-realized master carries his or her conscious energy and, therefore, the mantra is called the conscious mantra. It can easily activate your dormant spiritual energy. Then meditation happens naturally and spontaneously. Through repetition of mantra, the mind is rendered calm and concentrated. Meditation is really a greater depth of concentration. Patanjali describes meditation as the uninterrupted flow of concentration of the mind on the object of meditation.

You may repeat the mantra loudly to gain the ability to concentrate. The repetition of the mantra must be rhythmic. Observing the rhythm makes your mind calm. Become aware of the meaning of the mantra. The mantra refers to your own "I"-awareness. Your "I"-awareness is called Krishna, Shiva, Shakti, Allah, Jesus, Buddha, or the Absolute Reality. In other words, during the mantra repetition, you are calling your own name, which is the essential nature of your Supreme Reality.

Repeat the mantra with your in-breath and out-breath. Just as ice melts into water, let your mind melt completely into such a repetition. This technique is considered the most powerful as it enables your mind to become thoughtless. As you dive deeper and deeper into your own being, you can experience the whole universe rolling into your consciousness. Gradually, you will become filled with the bliss of your innermost "I am" awareness. This "I am" awareness called *satchitananda* (existence-consciousness-bliss) is who you really are. This is real meditation.

The ecstasy you experience cannot be described. The sum total of pleasures of the whole world is nothing in comparison to the bliss derived through meditation. You do not have to believe; you can *know* this. Just as the fragrance of a flower spreads out naturally, the bliss that you feel inside during meditation spreads out to others, thus building a noble world.

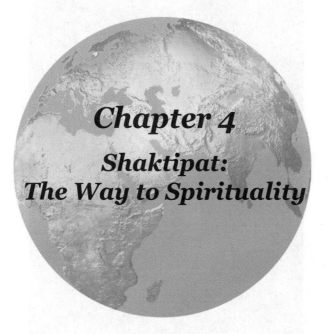

Chapter 4

Shaktipat:
The Way to Spirituality

Light destroys darkness

CHAPTER 4
Shaktipat:
The Way to Spirituality

An individual may be a true Guru, but he or she is not your Guru until you have received his or her *shakti,* which is a Sanskrit term meaning energy or power. The literal meaning of the word "Guru" is the dispeller of psychic darkness. Just as the darkness is dispelled when you bring light into a dark room, so also the Guru dispels the darkness that has been obstructing the passage to the highest consciousness within a human being.

Another meaning of the word "Guru" is mother. Like a mother, a true Guru gives birth; this birth takes place when an individual soul is united with the universal Spirit. With that union, a great experience happens, which may take you far away to a point where time stands still. In that union, you transcend both your physical body and mind, and experience absolute reality. That experience is transcendental. We know that hallucination does exist, but the transcendental reality also exists.

Once you have an experience of the transcendental reality, you are changed forever. The initial transcendental experience is known as *shaktipat.* It is in no way mesmerism or hypnotism because the effect of *shaktipat* is permanent. This transcendental experience may happen in thousands of different forms. Commenting on *shaktipat,* **Muktananda** wrote: "*Shaktipat* is a wonderful and mysterious spiritual process in which the Guru showers the energy of his own soul on the disciple. Without the grace of the *Siddhas, shaktipat* cannot take place. *Shaktipat* is a vast science. It is described in minute detail in the *shivagama* and *shaivatantra.* Books in Hindi include *Mahayoga Vijnana* by Yogananda Brahmachari and *Yogavani* by Shankar Purushottam Tirth. Books in English are *The Serpent Power* by Sir John Woodroffe and *Devatma Shakti* by Swami Vishnutirth."[78]

To explain who a Guru really is and what *shaktipat* means, I begin with my own experience.

1. Experiencing the Experiencer

I first met Muktananda (known as Baba) on Friday, September 13, 1974, at the auditorium of Northwestern University in downtown Chicago. When I entered the hall, Baba was already giving a lecture. At the end of the lecture, people began to form a line to meet him. I decided to join the line, thinking, "He's a saint, so let me ask for something that I really need."

As I came near him, Baba asked me my name and where I was from. After replying to his questions, I immediately said, "I don't have a job." At this, he raised his hand straight up in the air and said, "*mil jayega*" (you will get it).

The next day I returned for his program again and asked him, "Baba, when will I get the job?" This time he said, "You will get the job immediately after your *kundalini* is awakened. Take the program. It will be free for you."

The program took place on the evening of Monday, September 16, 1974. It was the most fortunate day of my life. I vividly recall this wonder-filled day at the Lake Point Tower in Chicago where Baba was conducting his public program. As was customary, men were seated on one side, and women on the other side of a middle aisle. Baba had just begun delivering his discourse with his opening statement: "Today's subject is meditation. The crux of the question is: What do we meditate upon?" In the hall packed to capacity, I was listening two times: first the words that Baba spoke, which were in Hindi, then their English translation by Prof. Jinendra Jain.

I was sitting at the corner of the middle aisle with my eyes closed, quietly aware of my breathing. Continuing his talk, Baba said: "*Kundalini* starts dancing when one repeats

Om Namah Shivaya." Hearing this, I mentally repeated the mantra, which was now fully charged with Baba's power of compassion. I noticed that my breathing was getting heavier. Suddenly, I felt a great impact of a rising force within me. The intensity of this rising *kundalini* force was so tremendous that my body lifted up a little and fell flat into the aisle; my eyeglasses flew off. As I lay there with my eyes closed, I could see a continuous fountain of dazzling white lights erupting within me. In brilliance, these lights were brighter than the sun but possessed no heat at all. I was experiencing the thought-free state of "*I am*," realizing that "I" have always been, and will continue to be, eternal. I was fully conscious and completely aware while I was experiencing the pure "*I am*," a state of supreme bliss.

Outwardly, at that precise moment, Baba delightfully shouted from his platform, "*mene kuch nahi kiya; kisiko shakti ne pakda*" (I didn't do anything. The Energy has caught someone.) Then he continued, "I [Baba] am like a radar. When something happens, I come to know of it immediately. He is a very good boy. He is highly educated. He comes from a very noble family. When the boy first met me, he told me that he did not have a job. So I told him that he will get the job immediately after his *kundalini* is awakened."

Baba noticed that the dramatic awakening of *kundalini* in me frightened some people in the audience. Therefore, he said, "Do not be frightened. Sometimes *kundalini* gets awakened in this way, depending upon a person's type."

In a short while, the brilliant white lights disappeared, giving way to a cooling experience. What a blissful cooling state, as if the coolness was coming from hundreds of moons! As I was still experiencing this ethereal state of indescribable inner bliss, Baba commented on the inner state that I was experiencing: "*Ab mere me aur isme koi antar nahi raha*" (right now, there is no difference between his state and my state). Kashmir Shaivism teaches that *kundalini* awakening may be experienced in any one of 27 different strengths—nine different strengths under each of these three levels: mild (*anavi*), moderate (*shakti*), and *intense* (*shambhavi*) — depending upon a person's type.

Baba then went back to his talk on the topic of meditation. Within me, the intensity of coolness gradually decreased. With the coolness coming down, I became aware of my physical body. I now realized that Baba had become my Guru the moment he made me experience the divine state.

With my heart full of great reverence and gratitude, I got up from the aisle and returned to my seat where a man gave my eyeglasses back. I was glad to find my eyeglasses intact.

Baba's talk on the topic of meditation soon ended. There was a short break before meditation. During this break, I walked up to Baba and prostrated myself at his feet. Baba's face lit up with ecstasy as he patted me on the back. "Read the book *Guru*. Tell your experience to others. That's why I wrote this book *Guru*," said Baba. (It should be noted that Harper & Row in America first published Baba's book *Play of Consciousness* under the title *Guru*.)

Meditation time soon began and all the lights were dimmed. Baba went around touching people with his peacock feathers. As he came near me, I heard him saying aloud: "*chup raho, chup raho, chup raho; abhi kuch nahi hona chahiye*" (Be quiet, quiet, quiet; nothing should happen to you now). Baba, being in full control of his own power, started to forcefully rub my forehead, right between my eyebrows. I sat silently the whole meditation time and felt thoroughly rejuvenated from within.

It is said, "*shaktipat ev diksha*" (*shaktipat* alone is initiation). **One who can give *shaktipat* initiation is called a true Guru.** *Shaktipat* Gurus are rare. The *Pratyabhijnahridayam* states, "*Madhyanadi vikasat chidananda labhah*," which means that only by receiving *shaktipat* through the Guru's grace is the central nerve unfolded, giving rise to the bliss of consciousness. The transmission of energy is not a religious phenomenon. Just as a seed contains a tree in tiny form and ultimately grows into a tree, the same can be said of what happens with *shaktipat* initiation. In the book *Devatma Shakti (Kundalini)*, **Vishnu Tirtha** observed: "We have pointed out repeatedly that no real progress in spirituality is possible unless an aspirant gets his *kundalini* power awakened, and it has also been pointed out that the easiest way of awakening that power is through initiation by *shaktipat* by a spiritual master."[79]

I used to visit Baba every day at Lake Point Tower to bow before him with my heart full of gratitude. Baba left Chicago on September 20, 1974. As Baba had predicted, I found an accounting position at CBS, a well-known television company in Chicago, on September 23, 1974.

2. On the Siddha Path

Following *shaktipat*, one becomes a seeker in the true sense of the term—seeking that awareness of the Self, which has been revealed by the Guru's power through *shaktipat*. I now became a seeker on the path of Siddha Yoga, a natural yoga that takes place only after *shaktipat* from a Siddha (perfect yogi). In fact, there can be no Siddha Yoga without the *shaktipat* initiation or rebirth. Did Baba keep count of that rebirth day? Exactly a year later on September 16, 1975, in Oakland, California, when I bowed before Baba, he said on his own, "One year is complete today."

The spiritual link is eternal. The Guru-disciple link can never be broken. If devotion to God cannot be changed, devotion to Guru also cannot be changed. It is devotion that really counts, not any physical form. Actually, a great transformation has taken place inside me, changing the way I view the world and myself. It is as though this outside world remains the same, but the prescription of my eyeglasses has changed. This world now appears as Consciousness, which exists everywhere within everything. Just as the same water is called by different names in different languages, so also the same Consciousness is called by different names in different

Narayan Swami (1909–1973)

religions.

Four years later, I visited Baba's main ashram in Ganeshpuri, India, for the first time. Before I left the ashram, on June 10, 1978, Baba said, "*Dhandhe ke saath saath Chicago mein swatantra center karo.*" (Alongside your business, open an independent center in Chicago). Then he gave me a shawl, which I still have as his precious gift.

On this *Siddha* path, I frequently see a tiny blue light called the blue pearl. Sometimes I see it with my eyes shut and at other times with my eyes open. This has been happening ever since that rebirth and it continues to be my most sublime experience. It makes me feel my beloved Baba's presence. Remember, it is this divine blue light in the crown of our head that makes us appear so dear to others. Once this tiny blue light leaves our physical body, no one would even want to look at us.

Now I can say with firm conviction that the "I am" awareness is the Spirit, soul or the inner Self, and it exists in everyone and everything. Undoubtedly, I am the Spirit. Both my mind and my physical body are simply the coverings over my Spirit, just as this shirt and coat are coverings over my physical body. To turn inward, toward the Spirit, is spirituality. To turn outward, toward matter, is materialism. Deep down within me, I realize that "I am" awareness can never die; it will continue to exist even after the death of my physical body. Just as rising and setting do not exist in the sun, birth and death do not exist in "I am" awareness.

3. Importance of a True Guru

All attainments automatically come from obeying the Guru. **Narayan Swami** (1909–1973) of Muzzafarnagar, a great spiritual master, said: "Whatever Guru says is higher than any Scripture (because it contains his power, and because it is specific for the disciple, rather than something general for all mankind)."[80]

Who is a true Guru? *Shiva Sutra Vimarshini* states: "*Guru paramesvari anugrahika shakti,*" which means that the true Guru is the grace-bestowing **power** (*shakti*) of God. The true Guru (called *Sadguru* or *Satguru*) is the Power that never dies. This Power can be transmitted through *shaktipat* by look, touch, sound, or thought. There are two terms: *Sadguru* and Guru. The inner Guru is called *Sadguru* whereas the outer Guru is simply called Guru. The outer Guru is needed in order to realize the inner Guru.

Sri Guru Gita, a sacred hymn in the *Skanda Purana*, fully describes what a true Guru is, and its recitation invokes a divine state within. The true Guru is within each of us.

It is said, "*Saktipatasca vedhakaksamasca guruh,*" meaning the Guru is one who transmits his *shakti* into the disciple and who can thus cause the disciple's *chakras* (energy centers in the subtle body) to be pierced. One becomes a disciple of a Guru only after receiving this *shaktipat* initiation, not before.

According to Kashmir Shaivism, God performs five functions: He creates the universe, He preserves it, He dissolves it, He conceals it within His own being to create it again, and He transmits divine grace to individual souls so that they can realize their oneness with Him. It is this fifth function — grace-transmitting power (*shakti*) — that is called the true Guru. In other words, the power is called the true Guru. When this power flows through a particular individual, that individual is addressed as a Guru.

The true Guru is *satchidananda* — Existence, Consciousness, and Bliss — seated in every heart. In fact, the true Guru refers to the one and the same consciousness called Christ consciousness, Buddha consciousness, Krishna consciousness, Guru consciousness, or Universal consciousness. "The Guru is in me, I am in the Guru" is the highest understanding.

It is said that enlightenment is possible only by spiritual birth from a Guru. A Guru is necessary for divine initiation. Indeed, having a true Guru is a greater accomplishment than any academic or worldly achievement. The Guru is one who points out to you that you are the Self. He makes you experience your own essential nature. I have heard the following story that reveals the importance of a Guru.

Once upon a time, a washerman went into a forest with his donkeys. There he saw a lion cub alone, without its mother, so he took the cub home, and he brought it up himself, along with his donkeys. The lion cub grew up with donkeys and, of course, he thought he was a donkey, too. One day the washerman took him to the river with the other donkeys, and while they were there, a grown-up lion happened to come along. He was amazed to see the young lion there with all the donkeys.

"What are you doing hanging around with all these donkeys?" he asked.

The young lion was surprised to hear this question. "They are my brothers," the young lion said. "I'm a donkey myself."

"Do I look like a donkey?" the old lion asked.

"No, you obviously belong to some other species," replied the young lion.

"Okay, let me show you something," said the old lion.

He took the young lion to the riverbank, and he pointed to their two reflections in the water. "Now, do you belong to their species or mine?" he asked and let out a tremendous roar.

Hearing the lion's roar, the cub tried to roar and found that he could! Filled with delight and wonder, the cub jumped, roared, and relished the realization that he was truly a lion. Immediately, the young lion began to live like a lion, eventually becoming the king of the forest.

That young lion was a lion throughout his life. He was a lion even when he thought he was a donkey, but it took an experienced lion to remove his ignorance. Without that old lion to point it out to him, that young lion might not have realized his lionhood. In the same way, the energy called *kundalini* in yoga is dormant within us. Only when the Guru's own energy enters into us to awaken the dormant *kundalini* energy, can we experience our own divinity.

Generally, one keeps one's own divine experiences secret from others, but remembering Baba's words, "Tell your experience to others," I have shared my experience here. I hope this record of what I experienced within inspires your faith in spirituality and guides the course of future generations. Let me now conclude with four authoritative quotations that may deepen your understanding of spirituality.

> In the *sahasrara* [The topmost spiritual center in the crown of the head], there is divine effulgence; that light has the radiance of a thousand suns. In that center there is no pain and no pleasure—only the bliss of Consciousness exists there. In the center of that divine effulgence in the *sahasrara* there is a tiny subtle blue light, which *yogins* call the *nilabindu*, the Blue Pearl. Watching this tender, infinitely fascinating light, you become aware of your true glory. Though smaller than a sesame seed, the Blue Pearl contains the entire universe. It is the light of God, the form of God within you. This is the divinity; this is the greatness that lies within a human being. This is the true wonder of humanity. Therefore, perceive that light. Just by looking at your face in the mirror, you will never know yourself. Only if you discover that light will you recognize who you really are. It was after seeing that light that the great ecstatic being Mansur Mastana said, "*anal-Haqq*," I am God. After seeing that, the great Shankaracharya said, "I am Brahman, I am the Absolute." With the awareness of that, Jesus said, "The kingdom of God is within." God's kingdom does not lie only within Jesus or within these other great beings—it is inside you and inside me and inside everyone.

> —From *I Am That* by Swami Muktananda (SYDA Foundation, South Fallsburg, New York), p. 60.

Religion, which is the highest knowledge and the highest wisdom, cannot be bought, nor can it be acquired from books. You may thrust your head into all the corners of the world, you may explore the Himalayas, the Alps, and the Caucasus, you may sound the bottom of the sea and pry into every nook of Tibet and the desert of Gobi, you will not find it anywhere until your heart is ready for receiving it and your teacher has come. And when that divinely appointed teacher comes, serve him with childlike confidence and simplicity, freely open your heart to his influence, and see in him God manifested. Those who come to seek truth with such a spirit of love and veneration, to them the Lord of Truth reveals the most wonderful things regarding truth, goodness, and beauty.

—From *The Complete Works of Swami Vivekananda Volume 3*, by Swami Vivekananda (Advaita Ashram, Champawat, India), pp. 52–53.

The Guru radiates power, peace, joy and bliss to the student in response to his thoughts. He is bathed in the powerful current of magnetism. The stream of spiritual electricity flows steadily from the preceptor to his disciple, just as oil flows from one vessel to another. The student can imbibe or draw from his teacher in proportion to his degree of faith. Whenever the student sincerely meditates upon his teacher, the teacher also actually feels that a current of prayer or sublime thoughts proceeds from his student and touches his heart. He who has the inner astral sight can clearly visualize a thin line of bright light between the disciple and the teacher, which is caused by the movement of the vibrations of *sattvic* thoughts, in the ocean of *Chitta*.

—From *Concentration and Meditation* by Swami Sivananda (Divine Life Society, Tehri-Garhwal, U.P., India), pp 67–68.

As a general rule all persons are not capable of receiving this *shakti* even if a Guru so desires, but a person's receptive capacity can be gradually developed irrespective of sex, age, caste, creed or nationality. A person's receptive capacity can be gradually raised by pious deeds, pure thoughts, devotion to God and ardent prayers to Him and selfless service of parents, spiritually advanced persons, and Guru. Manifestation of *shakti* also varies with different persons according to one's habits, nature and way of living. Householders too gain through *shaktipat*, which in fact knows no barriers.

—From *Devatma Shakti (Kundalini) Divine Power*, by Swami Vishnu Tirtha (Delhi, India, Swami Shivom Tirtha, 1993), p. 78.

Chapter 5

In Discovering Who I Am, God Is Known

Am I the one who ages and dies? Who am I really?

CHAPTER 5
In Discovering Who I Am, God Is Known

The greatest wonder of the world is that God, who is present in all beings, appears to be absent. God has entered into the substance of this universe, just as salt dissolves into water. The totality of all forms constitutes God. Explaining the presence of God everywhere, **Muktananda** said: "In what form would you like to see God? He has taken the form of bread in this piece of bread—don't try to see Him as stone in bread. In fruit you should see God as fruit, in a tree you should see God as a tree, and in yourself you should see Him as yourself. Who says that God cannot be seen? Don't try to see Him as different from the way He has manifested Himself. Try to see Him as He is."[81]

In fact, this universe is nothing but God in manifestation. Just as an actor manifests on the stage as a beggar or a king, so also God manifests in every form throughout the universe. Manifestation, not creation, is a scientific fact. The Law of Conservation of Energy states that energy cannot be created or destroyed. Energy transforms itself into matter. Therefore, seeing God everywhere in the form in which He is manifest is completely rational. God, who is present in all places, at all times, and in all things, must be present in this place, at this time, and in this thing. So it follows that God is surely present within each of us. Indeed, a human body is the abode of God. Accordingly, each one of us deserves the highest respect. If God is not within, He is nowhere else.

1. Who Am I?

The fact that you can say "I am" implies that an energy or life force resides within you. You can never say: "I do not exist." You exist. Doubting one's own existence is impossible.

Therefore, recognize your own being first. Just ask the question "Who am I?" and then question whether God exists.

The life — call it energy, power, consciousness, being, or soul — that exists within the physical body is experienced as the "I am that I am" or "I am" awareness. This "I am" awareness is one's own true nature. It is referred to as the inner Self or *atman* in Sanskrit. This inner Self is spiritual, that is to say, it is an immortal core of every human being. It is not physical matter — it is indestructible and changeless. To experience this spiritual divinity is the main purpose of human life on this earth.

One does not have to hunt for the inner Self in places of worship. I am the inner Self. However, there is often a false identification of the pure "I" with the physical body and the mind. The mistaken identification of the inner Self with the physical body and the mind can be removed through a persistent inquiry into "Who am I?" Anyone can benefit from the following practice of Self-inquiry.

I have a physical body (*sthula sharira*) in which I experience the **waking state**. In this state, I identify myself as the physical body and I see material objects. When my awareness relates to material objects, it is called objective, but when it relates to my inner Self, it is called subjective. In the waking state, although both objective awareness and subjective awareness are present, the degree of subjective awareness varies from 0 to 100 percent. The state of zero percent subjectivity in the waking state is really the state of absolute unawareness. Illustrating the state of absolute unawareness, **Lakshman Joo** (1907–1991), one of the greatest spiritual masters of the tradition in Kashmir Shaivism, noted: "When they observe any object such as a pot they become completely one with that object and lose consciousness that they are the observers. In Saivism [Shaivism] we call this state *abuddhah*, the state of absolute unawareness."[82]

I have an astral body (*sukshma sharira*) or a "subtle garment" in which I experience the **dream sleep state**. In the dream sleep state, I become aware that I am different from the physical body, and I mostly experience impressions of the objective world. Like the waking state, the degree of awareness of one's own subjectivity varies from 0 to 100 percent in the dream sleep state. The state of zero percent subjectivity in the dream sleep state is called the state of absolutely dispersed consciousness. Illustrating the state of absolutely dispersed consciousness, **Lakshman Joo** noted: "You see a pencil, then you see a book, then you fly in the air, then you are driving a motor car and yet you are not aware of any of this. You feel that everything is perfectly alright. In our Saivism [Shaivism] this state is called *suviksiptam*, absolutely dispersed consciousness."[83]

I have a causal body (*karana sharira*) or a "subtlest garment" in which I experience the **dreamless sleep state** when both the waking and the dream states disappear. I enter into a state of voidness or absolute silence. Although the mind becomes quiet, the breath does not stop. The degree of awareness of one's own subjectivity can vary from 0 to 100 percent in the dreamless sleep state.

These three states of mind—waking (in a physical body), dream sleep (in a dream body), and dreamless sleep (in a causal body)—are only passing states. The subjective "I am" awareness called existence—consciousness—bliss is the one constant that exists in all three states. In other words, when I say I am awake, I had a dream, or I was in dreamless sleep, I admit my continued existence in all the three states. That which is continuous is permanent. Just as a screen in a movie theater is the permanent background on which moving images appear and disappear, the "I am" awareness is the permanent background upon which all the three states of the mind come and go. Truly speaking, the "I am" awareness is only one state.

The awareness of "I am" is the basic fact of life. If we miss it, we miss everything. Forgetfulness of one's own Self is called the darkness of ignorance. Therefore, ask yourself questions such as: Am I the one who ages and dies? Where was I before I was born? Will I continue to exist even after the death of my physical body? Who am I, really?

2. Am I the Physical Body?

My physical body is composed of a brain, heart, lungs, digestive system, muscles, nerves, bones, marrow, blood, skin, and so on. Fundamentally, the physical body is made of the five basic elements of Nature: earth, water, fire, air, and ether. The hardness of my body is due to earth; the fluidity is due to water; the warmth that I feel in my body is due to fire; movement is due to air; and space is due to ether.

My physical body did not exist before its conception. Upon death, it will become a lifeless corpse. "I am" awareness is totally separate from the physical body for the simple reason that "I am" awareness is what perceives the physical body. I cannot be what I perceive. For example, when I look at a picture, I cannot be the picture. The very mention of the word **my** — my ears, my nose, my eyes, or my hands — proves that "I am" is separate from my physical body. The physical body does not say: "I am." It is "I am" who says, "This is the physical body." While the physical body changes from infancy to old age, "I am" always remains changeless. Truly, I am not the physical body, but the physical body is mine.

This physical body can be compared to an overcoat of flesh and bones. If the physical body falls away, there is no loss of the "I am" awareness at all.

The belief that I was born on a certain date and at a certain place exists because most people wrongly identify themselves with their physical body. My physical body is like a car. If the car breaks down, it does not necessarily mean that something has gone wrong with the person inside the car.

The physical body receives its power from the mind.

3. Am I the Mind?

The mind is the real doer of all actions. What exactly is the mind? The faculty of willing, thinking, feeling, reasoning, fearing, and desiring is referred to as the mind. The total individual mind is called *antahkarana* in Sanskrit, which is made up of three components: *manas* (thought), *buddhi* (intellect), and *ahamkara* (ego).

Even though the mind is connected with the physiology of brain, it is not a product of brain. The mind has its own existence completely independent of the physical brain. The mind survives the death of the physical body, thus accompanying the soul on its onward journey.

Fundamentally, it is the "I am" awareness that becomes the mind when bound with the three primal qualities of Nature, called attributes or *gunas* in Sanskrit, meaning "that which binds": *sattva* (harmonious), *rajas* (restless), and *tamas* (dull). Everyone's mind is under the sway of these three attributes.

The mind operates at three levels of awareness: *jagriti* (waking state or **conscious**), *swapna* (dreaming sleep state or **subconscious**), and *sushupti* (dreamless sleep state or **unconscious**).

The mind controls the five organs of action: mouth (speaking), hands (grasping), feet (moving), anus (excretion), and the genital organ (procreation). It also controls the five sense-organs: ears (sound), skin (touch), eyes (sight), tongue (taste), and nose (smell).

The mind is matter, but it is very fine, even subtler than ether. The mind causes all thoughts to arise. In fact, thoughts are nothing but the ideas garbed in words. A thought is a dynamic force that travels through space at a tremendous speed. As the most subtle form of matter, the mind receives nourishment from the food that we eat.

The mind's perceptions may vary from individual to

Swami Sivananda (1887–1963)

individual. For example, the same woman is perceived by her boyfriend, father, and brother in a different way, arousing different feelings in each of them.

Miraculous or supernatural powers known as *siddhis* originate from the mind, not soul. In Patanjali's *Yoga Sutras*, a deep mental state of the mind known as *samyama* is achieved when *dharana* (concentration), *dhyan* (meditation), and *samadhi* (absorption) become one.

Man's mind is his own heaven or hell. It has no particular shape or size. The mind takes on the quality of whatever it constantly thinks upon. A mind constantly thinking of God becomes like God. Revealing this nature of the mind, **Sivananda** wrote: "The nature of the mind is such that it becomes that which it intensely thinks upon. Thus, if you think of the vices and defects of another man, your mind will be charged with those defects and vices at least for the time being. He who knows this psychological law will never indulge in censuring others or in finding fault in the conduct of others."[84]

Having discussed the nature of the mind, we can now examine it more deeply. Often the mind's thoughts are negative. Anger, lust, hatred, jealousy, and greed pass through the mind like dark clouds appearing and disappearing in the sky of the soul. As each thought arises, inquire: "To whom has this thought arisen?" "I am" awareness is the real watcher of the thought passing through the mind. Just as we can observe the movements of our physical body, so also we can observe the happenings of our mind. Whatever we can observe is an object. The mind is an internal object. When our mind becomes agitated, we should not think that we have become agitated. Just as our eye is not damaged when an object falls and becomes damaged, so also our "I am" awareness is not damaged when any content of our mind gets damaged.

It is the mind that experiences pleasure or pain. If the mind, which is the link between the outer physical body and the inner Self, is somehow cut off, there would be neither pain nor pleasure. For example, a man who is operated under anesthetic, experiences no pain even when his stomach is cut open by a knife. In spite of the patient's mind becoming unconscious during the surgery, the inner Self continues to keep his physical body alive. From this it logically follows that the inner Self exists independent of the mind. Therefore, when we speak of "my mind," we are really referring to the mind as an internal object that exists apart from our "I am" awareness, which is its perceiver.

The mind is mine but it is not who I really am. To realize who I am really, I must then go to the source of the mind.

4. I Am That

When I am in a dreamless sleep state, my mind becomes unconscious. Upon waking up, I remark, "What a deep sleep I had!" Who was awake during the dreamless sleep state to report the experience of such a deep sleep? This proves that "I am" awareness must have been present during the dreamless sleep state. "I am" awareness, which never sleeps, is evidence of the existence of the inner Self. Indeed, I am the inner Self that is ever present in my physical body and the mind. The inner Self is nameless, formless, and non-dual. I am that inner Self. Just as the moon reflects the light of the sun, so also the mind reflects the light of the Inner Self.

You may have observed that people die everyday, yet an individual remains indifferent to his or her own death as if he or she will live forever. Why is this so? It is because immortality is the soul's very nature. The inner soul is invisible and indestructible. The awareness of "I am" remains the same yesterday, today, and forever under all circumstances—I am, I was, and I will always be.

The Inner Self or soul is the Knower. Just as the experience of seeing proves the existence of the eyes, the experience of knowing proves the existence of the Knower. The Knower alone is real and eternal. It is the ultimate experience. I can "become" the Knower because I already am. **Rama Tirtha** wrote:

> "To stand outside the body and mind,
> Is the way to peace of every kind."[85]

The soul (Knower) is encased in three bodies — physical, astral, and causal. Both astral and causal bodies which contain all the desires, passions, anger, and various tendencies, survive the physical body at death. In the words of **Yogananda**: "At death the physical body is destroyed. The other two bodies, astral and causal, are still held together by desires and by unworked-out *karma*. The soul wearing these two bodies repeatedly reincarnates in new physical forms. When all desires are conquered by meditation, the three body-prisons are dissolved; the soul becomes Spirit."[86] **Yogananda** adds: "At physical death man loses his consciousness of the flesh and becomes conscious of his astral body in the astral world. Thus physical death is astral birth. Later, he passes from the consciousness of luminous astral birth to the consciousness of dark astral death and awakens in a new physical body. Thus astral death is physical birth. These recurrent cycles of physical and astral encasements are the ineluctable destiny of all unenlightened men."

5. How Can I Be Considered God?

Respiration, digestion, hair growth, blood circulation, heartbeats, and other involuntary activities continue during the dreamless sleep state because of the existence of the Power within. This Power that is in me is in essence the same Power in every human being. Thus, this all-pervasive unity forms the basis of universal love. **Vivekananda** observed: "The difference between man and man, between angels and man, between man and animals, between animals and plants, between plants and stones is not in kind, because everyone from the highest angel to the lowest particle of matter is but an expression of that one infinite ocean, and the difference is only in degree."[87] In fact, the same Power exists in all the bodies of different names and forms in this universe. Trees

The water in the bowl and the water in the river are the same.

grow, rivers flow, and planets move due to this Power. To illustrate, there are innumerable soul-waves in an Ocean of Spirit. They all appear to be separate from one another. Some are high, some are low. Because of the wind of desires, the soul-waves rise up in the Ocean. If the wind subsides, so do the waves. Therefore, the soul waves are not separate from the Ocean of Spirit.

The awareness "I am," my true nature, always exists. Just as electricity does not cease to exist when a light bulb is broken, so the power of awareness "I am" does not disappear when the physical body of a person dies. Since the Power of "I am" awareness never dies, it is indestructible and ever-present. God by definition is indestructible and ever-present. Thus, the Power of "I am" awareness itself is God. In other words, "I am," is essentially the Ocean. Indeed, in discovering who I am, God is known. There is no other way. There never has been and there never will be.

Mansoor, a famous Sufi master, used to repeat *analhak*, which means, "I am God." Essentially, God and the individual soul are the same, as explained in the following dialogue:

Disciple: "Infinite worlds exist within God. How can I be considered God?"

Master: "Take my water bowl to the river and fill it with water."

The disciple left for the nearby river, and in a few minutes returned with the bowl filled with its water.

Master: "This cannot be the water of that river. I told you to get water from the river."

Disciple: "Oh, yes, this is the water from the river."

Master: "But there are fish and turtles in the river, and there are no fish and turtles in this water bowl. How can this be the water from the river?"

Disciple: "But this is just a small amount of water. How

could this small bowl of water possibly contain all those things?"

Master: "What you say is true. Now take this water and pour it back into the river."

The disciple went to the river, poured the water back into it, and returned.

Master: "Don't all those things — fish and turtles — exist in that water now? The individual soul is like the water in the bowl. You see, the supreme soul, God, has the awareness that it exists everywhere, whereas the individual soul believes that it exists only from head to toe in the physical body. In reality, the individual soul and the supreme soul are not two different things. The difference is never of quality, but of quantity."

Soul, a conscious entity, is a drop of the Ocean of All-Consciousness. It is of the same essence as God. Commenting on the statement "I am God," **Rama Tirtha** said: "The truth is that Rama [Rama Tirtha], being a Vedantin (a Sufi), is convinced that there is nothing but God and that 'I am God, as all others are.' Reality is only one. God is infinite. That which is infinite cannot be rendered finite by anything separate from Him. He covers everything and therefore, it is not a sin to say, 'I am God.' But it is certainly a great sin to reject the Reality just to project yourself as separate from or other than God."[88]

6. "I Am" Is the Essence of Religion

Albert Einstein said: "If there is any such concept as a God, it is a subtle spirit, not an image of a man that so many have fixed in their minds. In essence, my religion consists of a humble admiration for this illimitable superior spirit that reveals itself in the slight details that we are able to perceive with our frail and feeble minds."[89]

The inner Self, which is alive in each of us, is also called the Holy Spirit. We have just to discover it, and to discover it, we must delve into our own being. Truly, one who meditates upon one's own Self is considered to have worshiped all the gods and goddesses. This is the secret of all secrets.

The Old Testament — Exodus 3:14 — declares, "I Am That I Am." Indeed, "I am" is the name of God.

Aham Brahmasmi, "I am the Absolute," declared the *Yajur Veda*.

The nature of "I am" is motionless. "Be still, and know that I am God." (Psalms 46:10)

One of the Ten Commandments of Judaism is: "You shall have no other gods before Me," in which Me is the absolute Me, the sense of "I am," which exists not only within you, but also within all. What deity is greater than the inner Self? If one tries to worship anything other than the inner Self, then that worship is futile.

In the New Testament, Luke 17:21, Jesus said, "The Kingdom of God is within you." Since God is within us, wouldn't it make sense to search and find God by turning within?

Kabir, a great saint, declared:

Your Lord is within you,
Like fragrance in the flowers.
Why, like a musk deer
Are you searching for musk
In the grass again and again?

[Musk deer is a deer whose navel yields musk. The musk deer attracted by its own scent searches for it in the forest. Little does it know that the source of this fragrance is in its own naval. So too God is within every being but we seek Him outside of ourselves.]

The *Taittiriya Upanishad* (II, 6) states, "Having created the physical bodies of all creatures, God Himself entered into them to make them alive and active."

The *Bhagavad Gita*, Chapter II: 23–24 states: "No

weapon can cut the soul; no fire can burn It; no water can soak It; nor can any wind dry It.... The inner soul is indestructible, all-pervading, ever calm, immovable, and everlasting."

Muktananda taught: "Understand your Self. See your Self. Seek your Self, and find your Self. Hari, Shiva, Shakti, Allah, Jesus, Buddha—all dwell within you. Kneel to your own Self. Honor, and worship your own Self. Meditate on your own Self. God dwells within you as You."

7. In the Beginning Was the Word

According to *Maitri Upanishad*, Om is the sound form of the Self. In other words, "I am" is represented by the sound "Om." The words omnipresent, omniscient, and omnipotent begin with "Om," the universal sound. In the beginning of this universe, God was in the form of Word, which means cosmic sound. The sound **Aum** (Om) is known as the Word in the Gospel of St. John: "In the beginning was the Word, and the Word was with God, and the Word was God." **Aum** is the original divine sound, the basis of everything in the universe. **Amen**, a slightly modified form of Aum, is found in the religions of Judaism and Christianity. In the religion of Islam, Aum is found in the modified form of **Amin**.

When asked by some Muslim representatives whether he could quote any reference to Om in the Holy Koran, **Rama Tirtha** replied: "In the very beginning of your Koran, at the top, there are three letters, Alif (A), Lam (L), and Mim (M). Can any one of you explain what these three letters mean? . . . Rama will tell you what they signify. Alif, Lam, and Mim are nothing but Alif (A), Wao (O), and Mim (M), that is, AOM or OM."[90] The Muslim representatives objected that the letter L is not the same as the letter O, but Rama Tirtha pointed out to them that in Arabic grammar, L is pronounced O when it falls between a vowel and a consonant, as in the names Shamsuddin, which is written Shamsaldin, or Nizamuddin, which is written Nizamaldin. Here L is in-between a vowel and a consonant and therefore it becomes silent, and gives the sound of the Arabic letter *pesh* (O or U). "Accordingly, Alif, Lam, and Mim give the sound of Alif (A), Wao (O or U), and Mim (M), i.e. AOM or AUM. This is nothing but OM."[91]

The sound "Om" is the natural sound of God. It is all-pervading and universal. According to the Vedas, everything came into existence from the sound "Om". In the words of **Muktananda**: "The power of the Word is so great that the entire universe was created from it. The Word, or sound, exploded and became ether, the vibrations of which created air. Friction in the air created fire. The vapor of fire became water, and sediment in water became the earth."[92]

Modern scientists are beginning to recognize, as ancient sages did, that the sound "Om" reverberates ceaselessly throughout the universe.

8. Secret of Self-realization

Self-realization is the continuous awareness of the inner Self. While the inner Self is always realized, it remains obscured for most people. The "I am" awareness can never be lost. Is there ever a moment when the inner Self is not present? The inner Self is present throughout the three states — waking, dream sleep, and dreamless sleep. Forgetting one's own inner Self is living in a state of ignorance. The removal of this ignorance is the way to Self-realization. This subtle point can be grasped from the following story:

Once a woman, who was wearing her most precious necklace, forgot she had it on. She began searching for it frantically and looked everywhere. Unable to find it she began visiting her friends asking if any of them had seen it. Finally, she ran into a friend who pointed to her neck, prompting her to touch the necklace that had been there the whole time. The woman was very happy to find her necklace. In fact, she had neither lost it nor found it. Before, thinking it was lost, she was miserable. Now she became happy.

Like the friend in the story who pointed out the necklace,

a spiritual master makes a worthy seeker experience the divine inner Self that has been forgotten. Commenting on how a spiritual master reveals this divinity, **Sivananda** wrote: "A Guru can awaken the *kundalini* of an aspirant through sight, touch, speech or mere *sankalpa* (thought). He can transmit spirituality to the student just as one gives an orange-fruit to another. When the Guru gives *mantra* to his disciples, he gives it with his own power and *sattvic Bhava* [pure intention]."[93]

Self-realization is entirely different from the intellectual understanding of who we are. Knowing means more than intellectual understanding. It means knowledge based on experience. Could we ever know the sweetness of honey if we do not taste it? The key to Self-realization lies in a Guru-disciple succession (*guruparampara*). For example, Nityananda imparted the divine experience of Self-realization to Muktananda, and Muktananda, in turn, to Chidvilasananda. Thus, all the power lies in the Guru-disciple lineage. A saint has summed up the secret of Self-realization as follows:

सफा से मिला तो सफा हो गया मैं ।

खुदि मिट गयी, खुद खुदा हो गया मैं ॥

safaa se milaa to safaa ho gaya mein
khudi mit gayi, khud khuda ho gaya mein

"When I met a pure being, I became pure.
My ego no longer remained; I myself became God."

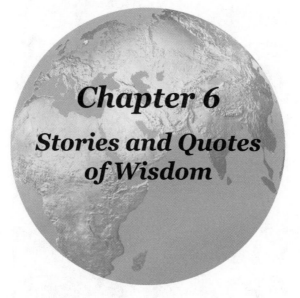

Chapter 6
Stories and Quotes of Wisdom

Six blind brothers washing an elephant.

CHAPTER 6
Stories and Quotes of Wisdom

When reason matures, it becomes wisdom. Just as knowledge is needed to pass the tests in school, so also is wisdom needed to pass the tests in life. The following are stories and quotes of wisdom intended to bring hope to the hopeless, joy to the depressed, and strength to the weak.

1. Harmony

Seeing a Part of the Whole Truth

The varying views of religionists are akin to the story told in India about six blind brothers who were washing an elephant. The first brother proclaimed that the elephant is like a huge wall; he had been washing the sides of the pachyderm.

Hearing this, the second brother disagreed, asserting that the elephant is like a flexible bamboo pole; he had been washing the trunk.

The third, thinking those two brothers were fools, insisted that the elephant is like two banana leaves; he had been washing the ears.

Hearing these absurd pronouncements, the fourth brother corrected them with his definition that the elephant is like a large fleshy roof supported by four pillars; he had been washing the legs.

The fifth brother laughed derisively, for to him the elephant was just two pieces of bone; he had been washing the tusks.

Now the sixth brother knew they were all crazy and declared definitely that the elephant was only a piece of rope hanging from heaven; he had washed the tail and, being the youngest and smallest, he couldn't reach the top of the tail and so assumed it descended from the celestial regions of the gods.

At the height of the quarrel, their sighted father arrived and explained, "You are all right, and you are all wrong. Right, because you correctly described what you experienced, but wrong because each of you experienced only a part of the whole. The elephant is an aggregate of all these parts."

— Excerpt from *Journey to Self-Realization* by
Paramahansa Yogananda, pp. 180–181

Credit: *Journey to Self-Realization* by Paramahansa
Yogananda (Self-Realization Fellowship, Los Angeles, USA)

I call myself a nationalist, but my nationalism is as broad as the universe. It includes in its sweep all the nations of the earth. My nationalism includes the well being of the whole world.

— Mahatma Gandhi (1869–1948)

My country is the world and my religion is to do good.

— Ralph W. Emerson (1803–1882)

It is steering, not drifting that can save any society.

— Rama Tirtha (1873–1906)

A community is adorned not by great men with small views, but small men with great views.

— Rama Tirtha (1873–1906)

Cooperation is better than competition.

— Rama Tirtha (1873–1906)

You may possess things, but you must not be possessed by them.

— Aurobindo (1872–1950)

True happiness lies in the finding and maintenance of a natural harmony of spirit, mind and body.

— Aurobindo (1872–1950)

Science without religion is lame, religion without science is blind.

— Albert Einstein (1879–1955)

You may fool all the people some of the time; you can even fool some of the people all the time; but you can't fool all of the people all the time.

— Abraham Lincoln (1809–1865)

2. Truth

Should I Speak the Truth if Another Is Hurt?

It so happened that once, when a monk was sitting by his little hut, a frightened man with a bundle ran past him and disappeared into a cave nearby. A couple of minutes later, there came a band of fierce robbers with gleaming knives, apparently looking for this man. Knowing that the monk would not lie, they asked him where the man with the bundle was hiding. At once, the monk, true to his vow of not uttering falsehood, showed them the cave. The cruel robbers rushed into it, dragged out the scared man, killed him mercilessly, and departed with his bundle. The monk never realized that he had been instrumental in the murder of a man. If by speaking the truth, another is hurt it ceases to be truth.

He who knows others is wise; he who knows himself is enlightened.

—Lao-tzu (604 BC–531 BC)

By three methods we may learn wisdom: First, by reflection, which is noblest; second, by imitation, which is easiest; and third by experience, which is the bitterest.

—Confucius (551 BC–479 BC)

The more I know, the more I realize I don't know.

—Albert Einstein (1879–1955)

I know nothing except the fact of my ignorance.

—Socrates (469BC–399 BC)

Watch your thoughts; they become your words.
Watch your words; they become your actions.
Watch your actions; they become your habits.
Watch your habits; they become your character.
Watch your character; for it will become your destiny.

—*Hillel*, also called Hillel the Elder, (60 BC–9 AD)

Wisdom has been defined as knowing what one ought to do next. Virtue is doing it.

—Rama Tirtha (1873–1906)

Men are not influenced by things, but by their thoughts about things.

—Rama Tirtha (1873–1906)

Dirt is riches in the wrong place.

—Rama Tirtha (1873–1906)

Man's highest faculty is not reason but intuition.

—Yogananda (1893–1952)

3. Nonviolence

The Sinner of Today Is the Saint of Tomorrow

Once a woman was charged for adultery. The Pharisees wanted Jesus to pronounce the Mosaic verdict of stoning her to death. Lord Jesus quietly said, "Let him that is without sin among you cast the first stone at her." This powerful utterance of the Lord at once turned the gaze of each one present within himself. Who could be without sin? Introspection revealed their own defects. One by one the people hung their heads down and left the place.

"Where are they?" Jesus asked the woman after some time.

"Did no man condemn thee?"

"No, my Lord," she answered.

"Neither do I condemn thee. Go thy way and sin no more," said the Lord, summing up in this beautiful incident the very essence of his divine message.

— Excerpt: *Kingly Science Kingly Secret* by Swami Sivananda, p. 91

Credit: *Kingly Science Kingly Secret* by Swami Sivananda, The Divine Life Society, Tehri-Garhwal, India)

By Saving an Animal, Lincoln Helped Himself

The American President Abraham Lincoln was once going to the Senate House. On his way he saw a pig in the marshes. The more the pig tried to extricate himself, the deeper he went. The President immediately ran to save the pig. In his soiled clothes he, thereafter, went to the Senate house. The senators were taken aback. The President narrated the entire incident to set their doubts at rest. They started praising the President for his kindness. He told them not to do so, because he had not, in fact, shown any mercy on the pig. He was pained to see the pig thus suffering. By helping the pig out of the marsh, he had only relieved himself of his affliction. He said that he was helping himself and not the pig.

—Excerpt *In Woods of God-Realization, Volume IV* by Swami Rama Tirtha, p. 202

Credit; *In Woods of God-Realization, Volume IV* by Swami Rama Tirtha (Swami Rama Tirtha Pratisthan, Lucknow, India)

Do Animals Have a Soul?

Try to understand. The animal is eating, you are eating; the animal is sleeping, you are sleeping; the animal is defending, you are defending; the animal is having sex, you are having sex; the animals have children, you have children; they have a living place, you have a living place. If the animal's body is cut, there is blood; if your body is cut, there is blood. So, all these similarities are there. Now, why do you deny this one similarity, the presence of the soul? This is not logical. You have studied logic? In logic there is something called analogy. Analogy means drawing a conclusion by finding many points of similarity. If there are so many points of similarity between human beings and animals, why deny one similarity? That is not logic. That is not science.

—Excerpt *The Science of Self Realization* by Swami Prabhupada, p. 32

Credit: *The Science of Self Realization* by Swami Prabhupada (International Society for Krishna Consciousness, Los Angeles, CA)

I do not want to make my stomach a graveyard of dead animals.

—George Bernard Shaw (1856–1950)

I do believe that all God's creatures have the right to live as much as we have. Instead of prescribing the killing of the so-called injurious fellow creatures of ours as a duty, if men of knowledge had devoted their gift to discovering ways of dealing with them otherwise than by killing them, we would be living in a world befitting our status as men–animals endowed with reason and the power of choosing between good and evil, right and wrong, violence and nonviolence, truth and untruth.

—Mahatma Gandhi (1869–1948)

The more weapons of violence, the more misery to mankind. The triumph of violence ends in a festival of mourning.

—Lao-tzu (604 BC–531 BC)

I know not with what weapons World War III will be fought, but World War IV will be fought with sticks and stones.

—Albert Einstein (1879–1955)

It is better to light one candle than to curse the darkness.

—Author unknown

Nonviolence has come among men and it will live. It is the harbinger of the peace of the world.

—Mahatma Gandhi (1869–1948)

Peace cannot be kept by force. It can only be achieved by understanding.

—Albert Einstein (1879–1955)

No one is reformed through threats and punishments because they compel.

—Rama Tirtha (1873–1906)

Peace in the heart makes us fit to survive.

—Rama Tirtha (1873–1906)

"Thou shalt not kill" is one of the Ten Commandments corresponding to the Vedic Dharma — *"Ahinsa paromo dharma"* —non-hurting is the highest religion.

—Vishnu Tirtha (1895–1969)

War and crime never pay. The billions of dollars that went up in the smoke of explosive nothingness would have been sufficient to have made a new world, one almost free from disease and completely free from poverty.

—Yogananda (1893–1952)

God chooses those who choose Him.

—Yogananda (1893–1952)

God is Eternal Bliss.

—Yogananda (1893–1952)

When you truly love God you will see Him in each face, and will know what it means to love all.

—Yogananda (1893–1952)

What lies behind us, and what lies before us, are tiny matters compared to what lies within us.

—Ralph W. Emerson (1873–1906)

4. Love

The heart is the hub of all the sacred places. Go there and roam in it.

—Nityananda of Ganeshpuri (1896? –1961)

The consciousness in you and the consciousness in me, apparently two, really one, seek unity and that is love.

— Nisargadatta Maharaj (1897–1981)

Let not a man glory in this, that he love his country;
Let him rather glory in this, that he love his kind.

— Persian proverb

In the Scriptures, love is considered to be God. Love is within all. Whoever loves himself loves God. That is worship, yoga and meditation. Moreover, love of the Self is also love of the world. It is the worship of the world as well as worship of all religions.

— Muktananda (1908–1982)[11]

I love my family more than myself, country more than family, and world more than country.

— Rama Tirtha (1873–1906)

A good life is one inspired by love and guided by knowledge.

— Bertrand Russell (1872–1970)

What we are is God's gift to us. What we become is our gift to God.

— Louis Nizer (1902–1994)

When you are born, you cry and the world rejoices. Live your life so that when you die, the world cries and you rejoice!

— Unknown

Give a man a fish and he eats for a day. Teach him to fish and he eats for a lifetime.

— Native American Proverb

Does God Listen to Our Prayers?

Questioner: Considering the vastness of the universe, with its countless number of galaxies, it is hard to believe that the Creator of such immensity would listen to our prayers.

Master: Your conception of Infinity is too finite! Although the Lord is infinitely vast, He is also, in His infinity, infinitesimal. Infinity means, "Without end." The Infinity of God's consciousness goes not only outward, but also inward—to the very heart of every atom. He is as conscious of every human thought as He is of the movements of the galaxies in space.

5. Guru

God sends the seeker indirect guidance at first through books and lesser teachers. Only when the desire for Him is very strong does He send help in the form of a Self-realized Guru. It is no favor to the Guru if the student accepts him. Rather, the student must have prayed very hard, in this lifetime and in former lives, to have earned so great a blessing.

—Yogananda (1893–1952)

Alexander Meets More Than His Match

Interesting stories have been minutely recorded by Greek historians and others who accompanied or followed after Alexander in his expedition to India. The narratives of Arrian, Diodoros, Plutarch, and Strabo the geographer have been translated by Dr. J. W. M'Crindle[i] to throw a shaft of light on ancient India. The most admirable feature of Alexander's unsuccessful invasion was the deep interest he displayed in Hindu philosophy and in the yogis and holy men whom he encountered from time to time and whose society he eagerly sought. Shortly after the Western warrior arrived in

---

[i] *Six volumes on Ancient India* (Calcutta, Chuckervertty, Chatterjee & Co., 15 College Square; 1879, reissued 1927).

Taxila in northern India, he sent Onesikritos (a disciple of the Hellenic school of Diogenes) to fetch a great *sannyasi* of Taxila, Dandamis.

"Hail to thee, O teacher of Brahmins!" Onesikritos said after seeking out Dandamis in his forest retreat. "The son of the mighty God Zeus, being Alexander who is the Sovereign Lord of all men, asks you to go to him. If you comply, he will reward you with great gifts; if you refuse, he will cut off your head!"

The yogi received calmly this fairly compulsive invitation, and "did not so much as lift up his head from his couch of leaves."

"I also am a son of Zeus, if Alexander be such," he commented. "I want nothing that is Alexander's, for I am content with what I have, while I see that he wanders with his men over sea and land for no advantage, and is never coming to an end of his wanderings."

"Go and tell Alexander that God the Supreme King is never the Author of insolent wrong, but is the Creator of light, of peace, of life, of water, of the body of man and of souls; He receives all men when death sets them free, being in no way subject to evil disease. He alone is the God of my homage, who abhors slaughter and instigates no wars."

"Alexander is no god, since he must taste of death," continued the sage in quiet scorn. "How can such as he be the world's master, when he has not yet seated himself on a throne of inner universal dominion? Neither as yet has he entered living into Hades, nor does he even know the course of the sun over the vast regions of this earth. Most nations have not so much as heard his name!"

After this chastisement — surely the most caustic ever sent to assault the ears of the "Lord of the World," — the sage added ironically, "If Alexander's present dominions be not capacious enough for his desires, let him cross the Ganges River; there he will find a country able to sustain all his men.[j]

"The gifts Alexander promises are useless to me," Dandamis went on. "The things I prize and find of real worth are trees, which are my shelter, blooming plants, which provide my daily food; and water, which assuages my thirst. Possessions amassed with anxious thought are wont to prove ruinous to those who gather them, causing only the sorrow and vexation that afflict all unenlightened men."[j]

"As for me, I lie upon forest leaves, and having nothing to guard, close my eyes in tranquil slumber; whereas, had I anything of worldly value, that burden would banish sleep. The earth supplies me with everything I need, even as a mother provides her child with milk. I go wherever I please, unencumbered by material cares.

"Should Alexander cut off my head, he cannot also destroy my soul. My head, then silent, and my body, like a torn garment, will remain on the earth, from which their elements were taken. I then, becoming Spirit, shall ascend to God. He enclosed us all in flesh and put us on earth to prove whether, when here below, we shall live obedient to His ordinances; and He will require of us, when we depart hence, an account of our lives. He is the Judge of all wrongdoing; the groans of the oppressed ordain the punishment of the oppressor."

"Let Alexander terrify with threats men who wish for wealth and who dread death. Against the *Brahmins* his weapons are powerless; we neither love gold nor fear death. Go then and tell Alexander this: Dandamis has no need of aught that is yours, and therefore will not go to you; and, if you want anything from Dandamis, come you to him."

Onesikritos duly conveyed the message; Alexander listened with close attention, and "felt a stronger desire than ever to see Dandamis; who, though old and naked, was the only antagonist in whom he, the conqueror of many nations, had met more than his match."

---

[j] Neither Alexander nor any of his generals ever crossed the Ganges. Finding determined resistance in the northwest, the Macedonian army mutinied by refusing to penetrate farther; Alexander was forced to leave India. He sought further conquests in Persia.

Alexander invited to Taxila a number of *Brahmin* ascetics noted for their skill in answering philosophical questions with pithy wisdom. An account of the verbal skirmish is given by Plutarch; Alexander himself framed all the questions.

"Which be the more numerous, the living or the dead?"

"The living, for the dead are not."

"Which breeds the larger animals, the sea or the land?"

"The land, for the sea is only a part of land."

"Which is the cleverest of beasts?"

"That one with which man is not yet acquainted." (Man fears the unknown.)

"Which existed first, the day or the night?"

"The day was first by one day." This reply caused Alexander to betray surprise; the *Brahmin* added: "Impossible questions require impossible answers."

"How best may a man make himself beloved?"

"A man will be beloved if, possessed with great power, he still does not make himself feared."

"How may a man become a god?"[k]

"By doing that which it is impossible for a man to do."

"Which is stronger, life or death?"

"Life, because it bears so many evils."

Alexander succeeded in taking out of India, as his teacher, a true yogi. This man was Kalyana (Swami Sphines), called "Kalanos" by the Greeks. The sage accompanied Alexander to Persia. On a stated day, at Susa in Persia, Kalanos gave up his aged body by entering a funeral pyre in view of the whole

---

[k] From this question we may surmise that the "Son of Zeus" had an occasional doubt that he had already attained perfection.

Macedonian army. The historians record the astonishment of the soldiers as they observed that the yogi had no fear of pain or death; he never once moved from his position as he was consumed in the flames. Before leaving for his cremation, Kalanos had embraced many of his close companions but had refrained from bidding farewell to Alexander, to whom the Hindu sage had merely remarked:

"I shall see you later in Babylon."

Alexander left Persia and, a year later, died in Babylon. The prophecy had been the Indian guru's way of saying that he would be present with Alexander in life and death.

—Excerpt from *Autobiography of a Yogi* by
ParamahansaYogananda, pp. 445-449
Credit: *Autobiography of a Yogi* by Paramahansa Yogananda
(Self-Realization Fellowship, Los Angeles, USA)

APPENDIX A
Great Personalities

Abraham Lincoln (1809–1865), 16th president of the United States (1861–1865), was a man of great humbleness and superb intelligence. He is known as the greatest leader in American history. During his presidency, he issued the Emancipation Proclamation, allowing all slaves in the USA to become free people. Lincoln was the protector of what he called "the government of the people, by the people, and for the people."

Albert Einstein (1879–1955), a German-born American physicist, discovered the theory of atomic energy. He is known for developing special and general theories of Relativity. With a few equations, he banished from the universe every concept of fixed reality except the one constant of light (the speed of light being 186,282 miles per second in a vacuum). He was awarded the Nobel Prize for Physics in 1921 for his work on the photoelectric effect. Israeli officials offered him the presidency of Israel in 1952, but he respectfully declined.

Anandamayi Ma (1896–1982) is considered to be one of the greatest saints of 20th century India. Although she had little formal education, her spiritual insights were both amazing and profound. The former prime minister of India, Indira Gandhi, was a devotee of Anandamayi Ma. She taught that there is only one God and nothing else.

Aurobindo (1872–1950), one of the most influential spiritual figures of modern India, was a genius. He lived in England for fourteen years. He edited the English daily *Bande mataram* and wrote fearless editorials. He was a prolific writer over a wide range of subjects including philosophy, yoga, poetry, and human unity. In 1926, he founded the Sri Aurobindo Ashram in Pondicherry, India. His visions continue to inspire thousands of people all over the world.

Bertrand Russell (1872–1970) was a British philosopher and mathematician. He wrote on various subjects including education, history, politics, religious studies, science, and humanity. He was awarded the Order of Merit in 1949 and the Nobel Prize for Literature in 1950. He was known for his spirited anti-war and anti-nuclear protests and remained a prominent public figure until his death at the age of 97.

Buddha (560 BC–480 BC) is the title given to Siddhartha Gautama, who was a famous yogi born in India. Buddhism, based on the teachings of Buddha, is the fourth largest religion in the world. The meaning of the word "Buddha" is "enlightened" or "awakened" one. He was a son of a king. Buddha preached meditation, which involves emptying the mind of all thoughts to achieve inner peace and greater intuition. He put down priest craft and animal sacrifices. He spread the message of love everywhere. The very mention of his name is enough to arouse devotion in the hearts of millions of people throughout the world.

Carl G. Jung (1875–1961), one of the greatest modern psychologists, was born in Switzerland. He developed his theories called "analytical psychology" to distinguish them from Freud's psychoanalysis and Adler's individual psychology.

Chidvilasananda (1955–present), known as Gurumayi, is a renowned spiritual master belonging to the Guru-disciple succession of the Siddha Yoga lineage. At the command of her Guru, Swami Muktananda, she bestows the precious initiation called *shaktipat* to seekers all over the world.

Christopher Columbus (1451–1506), the famous Italian explorer, was the first European to discover the New World on October 12, 1492 while on a mission to find a shorter trade route to affluent India.

Confucius (551 BC–479 BC) was born in China. His original name was Kung Fu Tze. Confucianism, based on the teachings of Confucius, is the eighth largest religion in the world. Confucians strive for cosmic harmony by creating a society based on order and virtue. *The Analects*, a collection of the sayings of Confucius, treats mainly of social welfare, human peace, and harmony in society.

Dalai Lama (1935–present), Tenzin Gyatso, the Fourteenth Dalai Lama, is the world famous spiritual leader of the Tibetan Buddhist religion. He was only 2 years old when he was first recognized as the reincarnation of an earlier Dalai Lama. He remained the head of the government of Tibet until 1959 when the Chinese invaded, forcing him into exile. He now lives in India. In 1989 he received the Nobel Prize for Peace for leading the nonviolent opposition to the Chinese rule in Tibet. He stresses harmony among different religions.

George Bernard Shaw (1856–1950), a prolific Irish-born writer, is considered one of the most significant British dramatists since Shakespeare. He wrote many plays, including the masterpiece *Pygmalion*. Shaw is considered both a visionary and a mystic. He received the Nobel Prize for literature in 1925 for *Saint Joan*. Shaw helped not only reshape the stage of his time but influenced the minds of his own and later generations.

Guru Nanak (1469–1539) was the first of ten Sikh Gurus. Sikhism, based on the teachings of Guru Nanak, is the fifth largest religion in the world. As his teachings spread, he attracted a large number of devotees, whom he described as Sikhs, or learners. Guru Nanak taught meditation to strengthen a person's sense of God. He is widely venerated by both Muslims and Hindus, as well as Sikhs. His teachings are contained in *Japji*, an important part of the Guru Granth Sahib, the holy book of the Sikhs.

Herman Hesse (1877–1962), the German-born writer and winner of Nobel Prize for Literature in 1946, is most famous for his novel *Siddhartha*. He became a citizen of Switzerland in 1923. His philosophy of humanitarianism and his maxim "be yourself" became immensely popular during the 1960s.

Hillel (60 BC–9 A.D.), also called Hillel "the Elder," was born in Babylonia. He became the model of the ideal Jewish sage. Known as a man of great virtues, he deeply influenced the texture of Jewish life. He put together the book of Jewish law called the Talmud.

Jawaharlal Nehru (1889–1964), a world-renowned statesman, was the first prime minister of independent India. He was a Kashmiri Hindu *Pandit*. Because he was very learned, people often addressed him as Pandit Jawaharlal Nehru. Throughout his 17 years in office from 1947 to 1964, he was deeply involved in carrying India forward into the modern age of technological advancement. In foreign policies he was "neutralist" while his domestic policies included democracy, socialism, unity, and secularism. He was also one of the principal leaders of India's independence movement in the 1930s and 1940s. His daughter, Indira Gandhi, served as India's prime minister from 1966 to 1977 and from 1980 to 1984.

Jesus Christ (4 BC–29 A.D.) is called Christ, which means anointed one or Messiah. He was a Jew born in present day Israel. Christians regard Jesus as the Son of God on earth. Christianity, based upon the teachings of Jesus, is the largest religion in the world. Jesus' revolutionary message was to love one another as you love your own Self. Jesus Christ taught and exemplified the virtues of tolerance and forgiveness, rather than revenge and hatred. The birth of Jesus Christ is so great an event in human history that time began to be measured from his birth year using the Gregorian calendar. The twenty-seven books of the New Testament, upon which Christianity is based, were written on papyrus scrolls. After being accused of treason against Rome, Jesus was sentenced to be crucified by the Roman Governor, Pontius Pilate.

Jimmy Carter (1924–present) was the 39th president of the United States (1977–1981). Following his presidency, Carter remained active in public life and gained new respect as an effective statesman and peacemaker, acting as a mediator in several international conflicts. He also used his influence as a former president to call attention to economic and social problems in developing countries and to promote human rights and democracy. In 2002 Carter was awarded the Nobel Prize for Peace for his accomplishments in these areas.

John Woodroffe (1865–1936) is the pen name of Arthur Avalon, an Englishman. During the British rule in India, he was the Chief Justice of the High Court in Calcutta. In the final years of his life, he lived like a Hindu Brahmin. His books, *The Serpent Power* and *Garland of Letters*, are known worldwide.

Kabir (1440–1518) was one of the greatest spiritual masters of India. People of both Hindu and Muslim religions became followers of the 'creedless' master Kabir. A weaver by occupation, Kabir ranks among the world's greatest poets. He is one of the most quoted authors in India.

Krishna (3228 BC–3102 BC), the eighth incarnation of the Hindu god Vishnu, came to earth in 3228 BC to kill an evil tyrant king named Kamsa. Krishna is not regarded a prophet of the Lord, but is the Lord himself incarnate. There are many legends surrounding Krishna's miracles described in *Shrimad Bhagvatam*. He is known primarily through the epic Mahabharata, in which he acts as the charioteer of the hero Arjuna. His discourse on duty and life to the warrior Arjuna just before battle against the Kauravas is famous as the *Bhagavad Gita*.

Kofi A. Annan (1938–present), a great son of Africa, was born in Ghana. He is the seventh Secretary-General of the United Nations and the first secretary-general to be elected from the ranks of the United Nations staff. In 2001, he received the Nobel Prize for Peace. He has used his good offices in several delicate political situations. He is fluent in English, French, and several African languages.

Lakshman Joo (1907–1991) was one of the greatest spiritual masters of Kasmir Shaivism. He was the disciple of Swami Mahatabakak in the line of great *Siddhas*. His wisdom drew seekers from around the world. He established the Ishwara Ashram Trust in India. His book *Kashmir Shaivism: The Secret Supreme* is a great boon to mankind.

Lao-tzu (604 BC–531 BC), the founder of Taoism, was born in China. He is famous for his scriptural masterpiece, *Tao teh Ching*, The Way and Its Power. His book breaks down false thinking. He represents the path of unorthodoxy. Literally, Tao is the way of ultimate reality. Taoists aim to balance the feminine side of the body called Yin with the male side called Yang.

Mahatma Gandhi (1869–1948), the most revered Indian leader in the world, unified people and freed India from Great Britain using the same principles of love and nonviolence as had been taught by Buddha and Jesus. Gandhi's doctrine of nonviolent protest to achieve political and social reforms will live forever. In his autobiography *The Story of My Experiments with Truth*, Gandhi has described his life with utmost frankness.

Mahavira (599 BC–527 BC) was a contemporary of Lord Buddha. Like Buddha, he was a prince by birth. At age 30, he renounced the throne to become a wandering ascetic. After more than 12 years of ascetic practice and absolute nonviolence he attained a state of omniscience. Jainism, based on the teachings of Mahavira, is the ninth largest religion in the world.

Mansoor (858–922), a famous Sufi master, who lived in Iraq and Persia, used to repeat *anal-haq*, which means, "I am God." He was hanged as a heretic for his pronouncement of *anal-haq*, which orthodox Islam of those days would not tolerate.

Martin Luther King, Jr. (1929–1968), an American Baptist minister who was honored with the Nobel Prize for Peace in 1964, led the civil-rights movement in the United States during 1950's and 1960's. His leadership ended the legal segregation of blacks in the U.S.A.

Max Planck (1858–1947), a German–born physicist, won the Nobel Prize for Physics in 1918. Without quantum theory, computers and cellular phones would not exist.

Moses, the greatest prophet of Judaism, received the Ten Commandments from God on Mount Sinai. His actual birth date is not known, but it is believed that he was born in Egypt in the 14th to the 13th century BC His life is known only from the Bible and the Koran. The first five books of the Bible, called Torah or Pentateuch are: the books of Genesis, Exodus, Leviticus, Numbers, and Deuteronomy. These are believed to have been revealed to Moses by God.

Muhammad (570–632), born in Mecca, Saudi Arabia, was the greatest Islamic prophet. Islam, based upon the teachings of Muhammad, is the second largest religion in the world. It is believed that God revealed the Koran to Muhammad to guide humanity to truth and justice.

Muktananda (1908–1982), the disciple of Bhagwan Nityananda of Ganeshpuri, India, was adept in giving the divine and rare initiation called *shaktipat*. Both the East and the West revered Muktananda as the Guru's Guru. Starting in 1970, Baba Muktananda traveled throughout America, Europe, Australia, and other parts of the world to give programs of meditation on the spiritual Self. Muktananda regarded all the major religions of the world as genuine. As a result, he did not create any new religion. Instead, he established Gurudev Siddha Peeth, a beautiful ashram near Mumbai (Bombay), India. And, to propagate meditation worldwide, he founded the Siddha Yoga Dham of America Foundation (SYDA) in the USA. In addition to his famous spiritual autobiography, *Play of Consciousness*, Baba Muktananda wrote several books including *Light on the Path*, *Mukteshwari*, *Reflections of the Self*, *The Perfect Relationship*, and *Secret of the Siddhas*.

Narayan Swami (1909–1973) of Muzzafarnagar, India, was extraordinarily learned — quite possibly the most learned man in India during the 20th century, not only in the Hindu scriptures, but also in every imaginable branch of knowledge.

As one of the greatest masters of tantra, he earned a great reputation in India as a man of vast powers.

Nisargadatta Maharaj (1897–1981) was a Self-realized master of India. Though brought up in poverty, he was the richest of the rich. He is known for his brilliant book, *I Am That*. Sri Siddharameshwar Maharaj was his Guru.

Nityananda (1896?–1961) of Ganeshpuri, Maharashtra, India, was the Guru of Swami Muktananda. He is known for his supreme spiritual realization. The temples of Nityananda — one in upstate New York and a second in Ganeshpuri, India — scintillate with great spiritual energy.

Patanjali, a contemporary of Lord Buddha, was a great sage. He is known as the highest authority on the practical science of yoga. His famous book, *Yoga Sutras*, is considered a complete book on yoga — so complete that no one can improve upon it. His *Yoga Sutras* is prescribed as a textbook for the systematic study of yoga.

Prabhupada, (1896–1977), founder of the International Society for Krishna Consciousness, was an extraordinary author, teacher, and saint. In the West, he preached continuously and wrote more than sixty books of transcendental literature.

Ralph W. Emerson (1803–1882), an American writer and poet, was influenced by Hindu philosophy. As a leader of the transcendentalist movement, he greatly influenced the religious and philosophical thoughts of his time.

Rama Tirtha (1873–1906), one of the greatest spiritual masters of India, was a brilliant mathematician. He took his M.A. degree in mathematics, and served as the Professor of Mathematics in the Lahore Forman Christian College. He lectured on Vedanta, the ultimate science of yoga in India, Japan, and the United States. His eloquence is captured in several volumes of his work *In the Woods of God Realization*. He was learned in Persian, English, Hindi, Urdu, and Sanskrit literature.

Rama, the seventh incarnation of Hindu god Vishnu, came to earth about 18.144 million years ago to kill the demon king Ravana. Rama is not regarded a prophet of the Lord, but is the Lord himself incarnate. His consort was Sita. He is the central figure of the Sanskrit epic poem the *Ramayana*. Great saints like Valmiki and Tulsidas have written about Rama.

Ramakrishna Paramahansa (1836–1886), one of the most revered spiritual masters of India, explored Hinduism, Tantrism, Christianity, and Islam, expressing that God can be realized through all religions. He was the Guru of famous Swami Vivekananda. He created the monastic order of Ramakrishna Mission.

Satyananda (1923–2002), a disciple of Sivananda, was a great spiritual master of India. He is remembered for his translation and commentary on Sivananda's *Brihadaranyaka Upanishad*. He founded the Bihar School of Yoga which serves seekers worldwide.

Sivananda (1887–1963) of Rishikesh, India, was one of the greatest yoga masters of the 20th century. Filled with a desire to pursue the spiritual path, he left his medical practice. His direct dynamic style of writing inspired seekers from all over the world. He founded the well-known Divine Life Society in 1936. He was a great blessing to humanity.

Socrates (469–399 BC), a great mystic from Greece, profoundly affected Western civilization through his influence on Plato. He achieved social popularity because of his ready wit. Socrates taught that we could not begin to understand the world around us until we understood our own nature. He stressed the worship of one Divinity instead of worshipping many gods. He was put on trial for corrupting youth with his non-traditional beliefs. He was put to death with a cup of hemlock, a fatal poison. It is Socrates who observed: "The unexamined life is not to be lived."

Sri Aurobindo (1872–1950) was a scholar, writer, poet, literary critic, philosopher, patriot, visionary, and yogi.

Born in India, he studied at Cambridge, England. During the revolution in India, the British put him in jail for his participation in the struggle for freedom. While in seclusion he underwent spiritual experiences which changed the course of his life. After his release from jail, he devoted his life to promoting a change in consciousness in India and the world.

Sri Chinmoy (1931–present) is a world-renowned spiritual master. At age 12, he entered the ashram of Sri Aurobino, where he studied for the next 20 years. In addition to discussing spirituality with world and community leaders, he has made creative contributions in the fields of music, poetry, painting, literature, and sports.

Vishnu Tirtha (1895–1969), a great spiritual master of India, is known for his book *Devatma Shakit*, an authority in the field of *shaktipat* initiation. His Guru was Yogendra Vigyani, the famous author of *Mahayog Vigyan*.

Vivekananda (1863–1902), born in Calcutta on January 12, 1863, was a prominent disciple of Ramakrishna Paramahansa. After the passing of Ramakrishna, he traveled to the United States, delivering his famous address at the conference of world religions held in Chicago in 1893. He is credited with making Vedanta popular in the West. In India he developed the Ramakrishna Math and the Ramakrishna Mission. He wrote a number of books including his masterpiece *Raja Yoga*.

Yogananda (1893–1952), the celebrated author of the book *Autobiography of a Yogi*, has inspired spiritual aspirants from around the world. A disciple of Sri Yukteswar Giri, he founded the world-renowned Self-Realization Fellowship in the USA. His message emphasized the unity of God within all religions. He was a very great yogi. His physical death on March 7, 1952, was marked by an extraordinary phenomenon. A notarized statement signed by the Director of Forest Lawn Memorial-Park testified: "No physical disintegration was visible in his body even twenty days after death.... This state of perfect preservation of a body is, so far as we know from mortuary annals, an unparalleled one.... Yogananda's body was apparently in a phenomenal state of immutability."

Zoroaster (630 BC–550 BC) was a great prophet in Iran. Zoroastrianism was founded on the teachings of Zoroaster. When still a fairly young man, he began receiving divine revelations from Ahura Mazda, a good spirit. His conversations with this godhead and his difficulties while preaching are recorded in the *Gathas*, part of the sacred scripture known as the *Avesta*, which explains the struggle between good and evil.

APPENDIX B
Universal Declaration of Human Rights

Source: United Nations Department of Public Information

On December 10, 1948 the General Assembly of the United Nations adopted and proclaimed the Universal Declaration of Human Rights. The General Assembly called upon all member countries to publicize the following text of the Declaration and "to cause it to be disseminated, displayed, read and expounded principally in schools and other educational institutions, without distinction based on the political status of countries or territories."

PREAMBLE

Whereas recognition of the inherent dignity and of the equal and inalienable rights of all members of the human family is the foundation of freedom, justice and peace in the world,

Whereas disregard and contempt for human rights have resulted in barbarous acts which have outraged the conscience of mankind, and the advent of a world in which human beings shall enjoy freedom of speech and belief and freedom from fear and want has been proclaimed as the highest aspiration of the common people,

Whereas it is essential, if man is not to be compelled to have recourse, as a last resort, to rebellion against tyranny and oppression, that human rights should be protected by the rule of law,

Whereas it is essential to promote the development of friendly relations between nations,

Whereas the peoples of the United Nations have in the Charter reaffirmed their faith in fundamental human rights, in the dignity and worth of the human person and in the equal rights of men and women and have determined to promote social progress and better standards of life in larger freedom,

Whereas Member States have pledged themselves to achieve, in co-operation with the United Nations, the promotion of universal respect for and observance of human rights and fundamental freedoms,

Whereas a common understanding of these rights and freedoms is of the greatest importance for the full realization of this pledge,

Now, Therefore THE GENERAL ASSEMBLY proclaims THIS UNIVERSAL DECLARATION OF HUMAN RIGHTS as a common standard of achievement for all peoples and all nations, to the end that every individual and every organ of society, keeping this Declaration constantly in mind, shall strive by teaching and education to promote respect for these rights and freedoms and by progressive measures, national and international, to secure their universal and effective recognition and observance, both among the peoples of Member States themselves and among the peoples of territories under their jurisdiction.

Article 1.

All human beings are born free and equal in dignity and rights. They are endowed with reason and conscience and should act towards one another in a spirit of brotherhood.

Article 2.

Everyone is entitled to all the rights and freedoms set forth in this Declaration, without distinction of any kind, such as race, colour, sex, language, religion, political or other opinion, national or social origin, property, birth or other status. Furthermore, no distinction shall be made on the basis of the political, jurisdictional or international status of the country or territory to which a person belongs, whether it be independent, trust, non-self-governing or under any other limitation of sovereignty.

Article 3.

Everyone has the right to life, liberty and security of person.

Article 4.

No one shall be held in slavery or servitude; slavery and the slave trade shall be prohibited in all their forms.

Article 5.

No one shall be subjected to torture or to cruel, inhuman or degrading treatment or punishment.

Article 6.

Everyone has the right to recognition everywhere as a person before the law.

Article 7.

All are equal before the law and are entitled without any discrimination to equal protection of the law. All are entitled to equal protection against any discrimination in violation of this Declaration and against any incitement to such discrimination.

Article 8.

Everyone has the right to an effective remedy by the competent national tribunals for acts violating the fundamental rights granted him by the constitution or by law.

Article 9.

No one shall be subjected to arbitrary arrest, detention or exile.

Article 10.

Everyone is entitled in full equality to a fair and public

hearing by an independent and impartial tribunal, in the determination of his rights and obligations and of any criminal charge against him.

Article 11.

(1) Everyone charged with a penal offence has the right to be presumed innocent until proved guilty according to law in a public trial at which he has had all the guarantees necessary for his defence.

(2) No one shall be held guilty of any penal offence on account of any act or omission which did not constitute a penal offence, under national or international law, at the time when it was committed. Nor shall a heavier penalty be imposed than the one that was applicable at the time the penal offence was committed.

Article 12.

No one shall be subjected to arbitrary interference with his privacy, family, home or correspondence, nor to attacks upon his honour and reputation. Everyone has the right to the protection of the law against such interference or attacks.

Article 13.

(1) Everyone has the right to freedom of movement and residence within the borders of each state.

(2) Everyone has the right to leave any country, including his own, and to return to his country.

Article 14.

(1) Everyone has the right to seek and to enjoy in other countries asylum from persecution.

(2) This right may not be invoked in the case of prosecutions genuinely arising from non-political crimes or from acts contrary to the purposes and principles of the United Nations.

Article 15.

(1) Everyone has the right to a nationality.

(2) No one shall be arbitrarily deprived of his nationality nor denied the right to change his nationality.

Article 16.

(1) Men and women of full age, without any limitation due to race, nationality or religion, have the right to marry and to found a family. They are entitled to equal rights as to marriage, during marriage and at its dissolution.

(2) Marriage shall be entered into only with the free and full consent of the intending spouses.

(3) The family is the natural and fundamental group unit of society and is entitled to protection by society and the State.

Article 17.

(1) Everyone has the right to own property alone as well as in association with others.

(2) No one shall be arbitrarily deprived of his property.

Article 18.

Everyone has the right to freedom of thought, conscience and religion; this right includes freedom to change his religion or belief, and freedom, either alone or in community with others and in public or private, to manifest his religion or belief in teaching, practice, worship and observance.

Article 19.

Everyone has the right to freedom of opinion and expression; this right includes freedom to hold opinions without interference and to seek, receive and impart information and ideas through any media and regardless of frontiers.

Article 20.

(1) Everyone has the right to freedom of peaceful assembly and association.

(2) No one may be compelled to belong to an association.

Article 21.

(1) Everyone has the right to take part in the government of his country, directly or through freely chosen representatives.

(2) Everyone has the right of equal access to public service in his country.

(3) The will of the people shall be the basis of the authority of government; this will shall be expressed in periodic and genuine elections which shall be by universal and equal suffrage and shall be held by secret vote or by equivalent free voting procedures.

Article 22.

Everyone, as a member of society, has the right to social security and is entitled to realization, through national effort and international co-operation and in accordance with the organization and resources of each State, of the economic, social and cultural rights indispensable for his dignity and the free development of his personality.

Article 23.

(1) Everyone has the right to work, to free choice of employment, to just and favourable conditions of work and to protection against unemployment.

(2) Everyone, without any discrimination, has the right to equal pay for equal work.

(3) Everyone who works has the right to just and

favourable remuneration ensuring for himself and his family an existence worthy of human dignity, and supplemented, if necessary, by other means of social protection.

(4) Everyone has the right to form and to join trade unions for the protection of his interests.

Article 24.

Everyone has the right to rest and leisure, including reasonable limitation of working hours and periodic holidays with pay.

Article 25.

(1) Everyone has the right to a standard of living adequate for the health and well-being of himself and of his family, including food, clothing, housing and medical care and necessary social services, and the right to security in the event of unemployment, sickness, disability, widowhood, old age or other lack of livelihood in circumstances beyond his control.

(2) Motherhood and childhood are entitled to special care and assistance. All children, whether born in or out of wedlock, shall enjoy the same social protection.

Article 26.

(1) Everyone has the right to education. Education shall be free, at least in the elementary and fundamental stages. Elementary education shall be compulsory. Technical and professional education shall be made generally available and higher education shall be equally accessible to all on the basis of merit.

(2) Education shall be directed to the full development of the human personality and to the strengthening of respect for human rights and fundamental freedoms. It shall promote understanding, tolerance and friendship among all nations, racial or religious groups, and shall further the activities of

the United Nations for the maintenance of peace.

(3) Parents have a prior right to choose the kind of education that shall be given to their children.

Article 27.

(1) Everyone has the right freely to participate in the cultural life of the community, to enjoy the arts and to share in scientific advancement and its benefits.

(2) Everyone has the right to the protection of the moral and material interests resulting from any scientific, literary or artistic production of which he is the author.

Article 28.

Everyone is entitled to a social and international order in which the rights and freedoms set forth in this Declaration can be fully realized.

Article 29.

(1) Everyone has duties to the community in which alone the free and full development of his personality is possible.

(2) In the exercise of his rights and freedoms, everyone shall be subject only to such limitations as are determined by law solely for the purpose of securing due recognition and respect for the rights and freedoms of others and of meeting the just requirements of morality, public order and the general welfare in a democratic society.

(3) These rights and freedoms may in no case be exercised contrary to the purposes and principles of the United Nations.

Article 30.

Nothing in this Declaration may be interpreted as implying for any State, group or person any right to engage in any activity or to perform any act aimed at the destruction of any of the rights and freedoms set forth herein.

NOTES

Chapter 1: Religiosity Divides, Spirituality Unites

[1] Paramahansa Yogananda, *Journey to Self-Realization*, Chapter "The Need for Universal Religious Principles" (Los Angeles, CA, USA, Self-Realization Fellowship, 1997), p. 181.

[2] Richard Lannoy, *Anandamayi, Her Life and Wisdom*, Chapter 6, "Discourse and Dialogue of Anandmayi" (Shaftesbury, Dorset, SP7 8BP, Great Britain, Element Books Limited, 1996), p. 136.

[3] Swami Rama Tirtha, *In Woods of God-Realization, Volume VI*, Chapter "Sanatana Dharma" (Lucknow, India: Swami Rama Tirtha Pratisthan, 1999), p. 263.

[4] Swami Muktananda, *Where Are You Going? A Guide to the Spiritual Journey*, Chapter "Sons of God" (Ganeshpuri, India, Gurudev Siddha Peeth, 1993), p. 167.

[5] Swami Sivananda, *Practice of Karma Yoga*, Chapter "Universal Laws : Law of Causation" (Tehri-Garhwal, U.P., India, The Divine Life Society, 1995).

[6] Paramahansa Yogananda, *Autobiography of a Yogi*, Chapter "Outwitting the Stars" (Los Angeles, CA, USA, Self-Realization Fellowship, 1998), p.187.

[7] Swami Sivananda, *Kingly Science Kingly Secret*, Chapter "The Mystery of Death" (Tehri-Garhwal, U.P., India, The Divine Life Society, 1981), p. 79.

[8] *Teachings of Swami Satyananda Saraswati Vol. I*, Chapter "Reincarnation" (Munger, Bihar, India Bihar School of Yoga, Second Edition 1984), p. 304.

[9] Swami Muktananda, *Play of Consciousness*, Chapter "A Golden Lotus Falls on My Head" (South Fallsburg, New

York: SYDA Foundation; Reprinted in 2002 by Chitshakti Publications), p. 174.

[10] Paramahansa Yogananda, *Man's Eternal Quest*, Chapter "Will Jesus Reincarnate Again?" (Los Angeles, CA, USA, Self-Realization Fellowship, 1988), p. 230.

[11] Swami Vishnu Tirtha, *Devatma Shakti (Kundalini) Divine Power*, Chapter "Idea of Moksha" (Delhi, India, Swami Shivom Tirtha, 1993), p. 32.

[12] Carl Jung, *Memories, Dreams, and Reflections* (New York: Pantheon, 1963) p. 323.

[13] Swami Vivekananda, *Raja Yoga*, Chapter "Reincarnation" (New York, NY, USA, Ramakrishna — Vivekananda Center of New York, 1982), p. 252.

[14] Paramahansa Yogananda, *Autobiography of a Yogi*, Chapter "Outwitting the Stars" (Los Angeles, CA, USA, Self-Realization Fellowship, 1998), p. 199.

[15] Paramahansa Yogananda, *Man's Eternal Quest*, Chapter "Will Jesus Reincarnate Again!" (Los Angeles, CA, USA, Self-Realization Fellowship, 1988), p. 231.

[16] Swami Sivananda, *Kingly Science Kingly Secret*, Chapter "Spiritual Evolution" (Tehri-Garhwal, U.P., India, The Divine Life Society, 1981), p. 86.

[17] Swami Sivananda, *Practice of Karma Yoga*, Chapter "Universal Laws: Law of Compensation" (Tehri-Garhwal, U.P., India, The Divine Life Society, 1995).

[18] Paramahansa Yogananda, *Journey to Self-Realization*, Chapter "Miracles of Raja Yoga" (Los Angeles, CA, USA, Self-Realization Fellowship, 1997), p. 319.

[19] From the "Kofi A. Annan Nobel Lecture" delivered in Oslo, on December 10, 2001. The 2001 Noble Prize for Peace was awarded jointly to the UN and its Secretary-General, Kofi A. Annan.

[20] Swami Vivekananda, *Raja Yoga*, Chapter "Dhyana and Samadhi" (New York, NY, USA, Ramakrishna — Vivekananda Center of New York, Paperback Edition 1982), p. 83.

[21] Swami Nikhilananda, *The Gospel of Sri Ramakrishna*, Chapter "Master and Disciple" (New York, NY, USA, Ramakrishna — Vivekananda Center, 1992), pp. 85–86.

[22] Swami Rama Tirtha, *In Woods of God-Realization, Volume VI*, Chapter "Sanatana Dharma" (Lucknow, India: Swami Rama Tirtha Pratisthan, 1999), p. 265.

[23] Swami Sivananda, *May I Answer That* (Tehri-Garhwal, U.P., India, The Divine Life Society, World Wide Web Edition: 1997).

[24] Swami Rama Tirtha, *In Woods of God-Realization, Volume VI*, Chapter "A Session with Muslim Representatives (Part-1)" (Lucknow, India: Swami Rama Tirtha Pratisthan, 1999), p. 219.

[25] Paramahansa Yogananda, *Journey to Self-Realization*, Chapter "Mahatma Gandhi: Apostle of Peace" (Los Angeles, CA, USA, Self-Realization Fellowship, 1997), p. 196.

[26] Paramahansa Yogananda, *Journey to Self-Realization*, Chapter "Nations, Beware!" (Los Angeles, CA, USA, Self-Realization Fellowship, 1997), p. 197.

[27] Paramahansa Yogananda, *The Divine Romance*, Chapter "The Mystery of Mahatma Gandhi" (Los Angeles, CA, USA, Self-Realization Fellowship, 1986), p. 124.

[28] Axis powers (Germany, Italy, Japan, Hungary, Romania, and Bulgaria) versus Allies (USA, Britain, France, USSR, Australia, Belgium, Brazil, Canada, China, Denmark, Greece, Netherlands, New Zealand, Norway, Poland, South Africa, and Yugoslavia).

[29] The devastation caused by atomic bombs forced Japan to surrender on August 14, 1945, thereby ending the Second World War, which began when Germany invaded Poland on

September 1, 1939.

[30] Swami Satyananda Saraswati, *Bhakti Yoga Sagar, Volume Three*, Chapter "Changing Social Codes" (Munger, Bihar, India, Sivananda Math, First Edition 1997), p. 98.

[31] Paramahansa Yogananda, *Journey to Self-Realization*, Chapter "The Need for Universal Religious Principles" (Los Angeles, CA, USA, Self-Realization Fellowship, 1997), p. 190.

[32] Tenzin Gyatso, "The Monk in the Lab," *The New York Times*, April 26, 2003, Section A, Page 19, Column 2.

[33] Swami Rama Tirtha, *In Woods of God-Realization, Volume III*, Chapter "An Appeal to Americans" (Lucknow, India: Swami Rama Tirtha Pratisthan, 1979), pp. 257–258.

[34] *Teachings of Swami Satyananda Saraswati Vol. I*, Chapter "World Affairs" (Munger, Bihar, India, Bihar School of Yoga, Second Edition 1984), p. 317.

[35] Swami Muktananda, *Meditate*, Chapter "Looking Within" by Gurumayi Chidvilasananda. (Albany, NY State University of New York, Second Edition 1991), p. 48.

[36] Swami Rama Tirtha, *In Woods of God -Realization, Volume IV*, Chapter "Experiences in the Foreign Countries" (Lucknow, India: Swami Rama Tirtha Pratisthan, 1993), p. 196.

[37] Paramahansa Yogananda, *Journey to Self-Realization*, Chapter "The Need for Universal Religious Principles" (Los Angeles, CA, USA, Self-Realization Fellowship, 1997), p. 190.

[38] Jawaharlal Nehru, *Glimpses of World History*, Chapter "The World of Ashoka's Time" (New Delhi, India, Jawaharlal Nehru Memorial Fund, 1999), pp. 65–66.

Chapter 2: A Call for Harmony among Nations

[39] Excerpts from Paramahansa Yogananda's article on "Preventing Wars" in *Inner Culture*, 1935-1942, re-published in *Clarity from Ananda Sangha*, a magazine of spiritual teachings and practices for everyday living, Issue Spring 2002, p. 11

[40] The lecture is known as "The Dalai Lama's Nobel Lecture" delivered at the University Aula, Oslo, on December 11, 1989. Dalai Lama was awarded the Nobel Prize for Peace in 1989.

[41] Mansergh, N.; Lumby, E. W. R.; and Moon, Penderel, eds. *India: The Transfer of Power Vol. X*: The Mountbatten Viceroyalty, Formulation of Plan, 22 March-23 May 1947 (1981), Letter dated May 8, 1947, (London: HMSO, 1970-1983) p. 667.

[42] *Basic Facts about the United Nations* (New York, NY, USA, United Nations Department of Public Information, 2000), p. 99.

[43] S.K. Sharma and Usha Sharma, *Dalai Lama and Tibet*, Chapter "China and the Future of Tibet" by The Dalai Lama (New Delhi, India, Anmol Publications Pvt. Ltd., First Edition 1997), p. 78.

[44] Jawaharlal Nehru, *The Discovery of India*, Chapter "New Problems: The Arabs and the Mongols" (New Delhi, India, Jawaharlal Nehru Memorial Fund, 1999), p. 238.

[45] Jawaharlal Nehru, *The Discovery of India*, Chapter "The Discovery of India: The Mahabharata" (New Delhi, India, Jawaharlal Nehru Memorial Fund, 1999), p. 107.

[46] Swami Satyananda Saraswati, *Bhakti Yoga Sagar, Volume Three*, Chapter "Historical Fact and Tradition" (Munger, Bihar, India, Sivananda Math, First Edition 1997), p. 135.

[47] Swami Satyananda Saraswati, *Bhakti Yoga Sagar, Volume Three*, Chapter " Historical Fact and Tradition" (Munger,

Bihar, India, Sivananda Math, First Edition 1997), p. 134.

[48] Swami Rama Tirtha, *In Woods of God-Realization, Volume VI*, Chapter "Sanatana Dharma" (Lucknow, India: Swami Rama Tirtha Pratisthan, 1999), p. 302.

[49] Paramahansa Yogananda, *Autobiography of a Yogi*, Chapter "The Years 1940–1951" (Los Angeles, CA, USA, Sel-Realization Fellowship, 1998), p. 557.

[50] Swami Rama Tirtha, *In Woods of God-Realization, Volume III*, Chapter "An Appeal to Americans" (Lucknow, India: Swami Rama Tirtha Pratisthan, 1979), p. 257.

[51] In a statement posted on the Carter Center website after Jimmy Carter was named as a recipient of the 2002 Nobel Peace Prize.

[52] Swami Rama Tirtha, *In Woods of God-Realization, Volume III*, Chapter "The Future of India" (Lucknow, India: Swami Rama Tirtha Pratisthan, 1979), p. 200.

[53] Swami Rama Tirtha, *In Woods of God-Realization, Volume IV*, Chapter "Talk at Faizabad" (Lucknow, India: Swami Rama Tirtha Pratisthan, 1993), p. 286.

[54] Swami Sivananda, *Kingly Science Kingly Secret*, Chapter "Unity of Consciousness" (Tehri-Garhwal, U.P., India, The Divine Life Society, 1981), p. 224.

[55] Sri Aurobindo, *The Essential Writings of Sri Aurobindo*, Chapter "Appendix: the Fifteenth of August 1947" (New Delhi, India, Manzar Khan, Oxford University Press, 1998), pp. 370–371.

Chapter 3: Yoga: The Highest of All Unions

[56] Paramahansa Yogananda, *Journey to Self-Realization*, Chapter "Miracles of Raja Yoga" (Los Angeles, CA, USA, Self-Realization Fellowship, 1997), p. 321.

[57] Sri Chinmoy, *Astrology, the Supernatural and the Beyond*, Chapter "Man and the Universe" (Jamaica, NY, Aum Publications, 1973), p. 110.

[58] Swami Muktananda Paramhansa, *From the Finite to the Infinite, Volume I*, (South Fallsburg, New York: SYDA Foundation, 1989), p. 39.

[59] Swami Muktananda, *Play of Consciousness*, Chapter "The Greatness of the Guru" (South Fallsburg, New York: SYDA Foundation; Reprinted in 2002 by Chitshakti Publications), p. 26.

[60] Swami Sivananda, *Kundalini Yoga*, Chapter "Introduction" (Tehri-Garhwal, U.P., India, The Divine Life Society, 1986), p. xxxix.

[61] Paramahansa Yogananda, *Autobiography of a Yogi*, Chapter "I Became a Monk of the Swami Order," (Los Angeles, CA, USA, Self-Realization Fellowship, 1998) p. 265.

[62] Swami Rama Tirtha, *In Woods of God-Realization, Volume III*, Chapter "World's Spiritual Debt to India" (Lucknow, India: Swami Rama Tirtha Pratisthan, 1979), p. 227.

[63] Swami Satyananda, *Teachings of Swami Satyananda Saraswati Volume V*, (Munger, Bihar, India, Bihar School of Yoga, First Edition 1986), p. 418

[64] Paramahansa Yogananda, *The Divine Romance*, Chapter "The Why and How of Religion" (Los Angeles, CA, USA, Self-Realization Fellowship), p. 74.

[65] Paramahansa Yogananda, *Autobiography of a Yogi*, Chapter "The Law of Miracles" (Los Angeles, CA, USA, Self-Realization Fellowship, 1998), p. 315.

[66] *The Complete Works of Swami Vivekananda, Volume 1*, Chapter "Raja-Yoga" (Champawat, India, Advaita Ashram, 1989), pp. 232–233.

[67] Swami Vivekananda, *Raja Yoga*, Chapter "Concentration: Its Spiritual Uses" (New York, NY, USA, Ramakrishna—

Vivekananda Center of New York, 1982), p. 103.

[68] Swami Rama Tirtha, *In Woods of God-Realization, Volume I*, Chapter "The Spiritual Power That Wins" (Lucknow, India: Swami Rama Tirtha Pratisthan, 1999), p. 202.

[69] Paramahansa Yogananda, *Journey to Self-Realization*, Chapter "Miracles of Raja Yoga" (Los Angeles, CA, USA, Self-Realization Fellowship), p. 324.

[70] Paramahansa Yogananda, *Autobiography of a Yogi*, Chapter "I Become a Monk of the Swami Order" (Los Angeles, CA, USA, Self-Realization Fellowship, 1998), p. 266.

[71] Paramahansa Yogananda, *Autobiography of a Yogi*, Chapter "I Became a Monk of the Swami Order," (Los Angeles, CA, USA, Self-Realization Fellowship, 1998) p. 266.

[72] *e.encyclopedia*, Chapter "Human Body" (New York, NY, USA, DK Publishing, Inc., First American Edition, 2003), p. 139.

[73] *Teachings of Swami Satyananda Saraswati, Vol. V*, Chapter "Yoga Research and Meditation" (Munger, Bihar, India, Bihar School of Yoga, First Edition 1986), p. 478.

[74] *Teachings of Swami Satyananda Saraswati, Vol. VI*, Chapter "Integral Yoga" (Munger, Bihar, India, Bihar School of Yoga, First Edition 1986), p. 71.

[75] "Just Say Om" by Joel Stein, *Time*, August 4, 2003, Vol. 162, No. 5.

[76] Paul Reps, *Zen Flesh, Zen Bones*, Chapter "Centering" (New York, NY, Doubleday, 1989), p. 161.

[77] Swami Muktananda, *I Have Become Alive*, Chapter "How to Meditate on the Self" (South Fallsburg, New York: SYDA Foundation, 1992), p. 60.

Chapter 4: Shaktipat: The Way to Spirituality

[78] Swami Muktananda Paramahamsa, *Bhagawan Nityananda of Ganeshpuri*, Chapter "The Power of Shaktipat" (South Fallsburg, New York: SYDA Foundation, 1996), pp. 49–50.

[79] Swami Vishnu Tirtha, *Devatma Shakti (Kundalini) Divine Power*, Chapter "Secret of *Upasana* (Worship)" (Delhi, India, Swami Shivom Tirtha, 1993), p. 129.

[80] Swami Kriyananda, *Letters from India* (Nevada City, California, Ananda Publications), p. 34.

Chapter 5: In Discovering Who I Am, God Is Known

[81] "From the Words of Swami Muktananda: Try to See Him as He is," *Darshan*, April 1997, Issue: 121 (South Fallsburg, NY, SYDA Foundation), p. 36.

[82] Swami Lakshman Jee, *Kashmir Shaivism*, Chapter "The Five States of the Individual Subjective Body" (Albany, NY, USA, The State University of New York Press under the imprint of The Universal Shaiva Trust, 1988), p. 73.

[83] Swami Lakshman Jee, *Kashmir Shaivism*, Chapter "The Five States of the Individual Subjective Body" (Albany, NY, USA, The State University of New York Press under the imprint of The Universal Shaiva Trust, 1988), p. 75.

[84] Swami Sivananda, *Concentration and Meditation*, Chapter "Theory of Concentration" (Tehri-Garhwal, U.P., India, The Divine Life Society, 1994), p. 23.

[85] Swami Rama Tirtha, *In Woods of God-Realization, Volume VI*, Chapter "Way to Peace" (Lucknow, India: Swami Rama Tirtha Pratisthan, 1999), p. 38.

[86] Paramahansa Yogananda, *God Talks With Arjuna*

The Bhagavad Gita, Chapter II (Los Angeles, CA, USA, Self-Realization Fellowship, 1996), p. 214

[87] *The Complete Works of Swami Vivekananda, Volume 1*, Chapter "Reason and Religion" (Champawat, India, Advaita Ashram, 1989), p. 374.

[88] Swami Rama Tirtha, *In Woods of God-Realization*, Volume VI, Chapter "A Session with Muslim Representatives (Part-1)" (Lucknow, India: Swami Rama Tirtha Pratisthan, 1999), p. 159.

[89] Peter A. Bucky, *The Private Albert Einstein*, (Kansas City: Andrews and McMeel, 1992) pp. 85–87.

[90] Swami Rama Tirtha, *In Woods of God-Realization*, Volume VI, Chapter "A Session with Muslim Representatives (Part-1)" (Lucknow, India: Swami Rama Tirtha Pratisthan, 1999), p. 144.

[91] Swami Rama Tirtha, *In Woods of God-Realization, Volume VI*, Chapter "A Session with Muslim Representatives (Part-1)" (Lucknow, India: Swami Rama Tirtha Pratisthan, 1999), p. 144.

[92] Swami Muktananda, *Conversations with Swami Muktananda*, Chapter "The Power of Words" (South Fallsburg, New York: SYDA Foundation, 1998), p. 16.

[93] Swami Sivananda, Kundalini Yoga, Chapter "Preliminary" (Tehri-Garhwal, U.P., India, The Divine Life Society, 1986), p. 21.

INDEX

D

E

F

G

H

I

J

K

L

M

N

Z